International Law
and the Status of Women

A Westview Replica Edition

The concept of Westview Replica Editions is a response to the continuing crisis in academic and informational publishing. Library budgets for books have been severely curtailed. Ever larger portions of general library budgets are being diverted from the purchase of books and used for data banks, computers, micromedia, and other methods of information retrieval. Interlibrary loan structures further reduce the edition sizes required to satisfy the needs of the scholarly community. Economic pressures (particularly inflation and high interest rates) on the university presses and the few private scholarly publishing companies have severely limited the capacity of the industry to properly serve the academic and research communities. As a result, many manuscripts dealing with important subjects, often representing the highest level of scholarship, are no longer economically viable publishing projects--or, if accepted for publication, are typically subject to lead times ranging from one to three years.

Westview Replica Editions are our practical solution to the problem. We accept a manuscript in camera-ready form, typed according to our specifications, and move it immediately into the production process. As always, the selection criteria include the importance of the subject, the work's contribution to scholarship, and its insight, originality of thought, and excellence of exposition. The responsibility for editing and proofreading lies with the author or sponsoring institution. We prepare chapter headings and display pages, file for copyright, and obtain Library of Congress Cataloging in Publication Data. A detailed manual contains simple instructions for preparing the final typescript, and our editorial staff is always available to answer questions.

The end result is a book printed on acid-free paper and bound in sturdy library-quality soft covers. We manufacture these books ourselves using equipment that does not require a lengthy make-ready process and that allows us to publish first editions of 300 to 600 copies and to reprint even smaller quantities as needed. Thus, we can produce Replica Editions quickly and can keep even very specialized books in print as long as there is a demand for them.

About the Book and Author

International Law and the Status of Women
Natalie Kaufman Hevener

Since 1945 more than 20 international legal instruments dealing specifically with women have been modified or consummated, reflecting a growing international consensus on issues concerning women's role in society. This book is the first complete collection and examination of this group of documents. Dr. Hevener analyzes each of the agreements and assesses its likely impact on the legal status of women. Categorizing the documents according to their goals, she demonstrates the broad range of economic, social, and political concerns they cover and evaluates contemporary patterns and future needs they reveal. The book includes a table of ratifications organized by country and region.

Dr. Hevener is associate professor in the Department of Government and International Studies at the University of South Carolina. She is editor of *The Dynamics of Human Rights in U.S. Foreign Policy (1981)*.

To Suzy

International Law
and the Status of Women

Natalie Kaufman Hevener

Westview Press / Boulder, Colorado

A Westview Replica Edition

Copyright © 1983 by Westview Press, Inc.

Published in 1983 in the United States of America by
     Westview Press, Inc.
     5500 Central Avenue
     Boulder, Colorado 80301
     Frederick A. Praeger, President and Publisher

Library of Congress Cataloging in Publication Data
Hevener, Natalie Kaufman
International law and the status of women
     (A Westview Replica Edition)
     Includes Index
     1. Women (International law)   I. Title.   II. Series.
K644.H48   1982   341.4'81   82-20298
ISBN 0-86531-924-3

10 9 8 7 6 5 4 3

Contents

ix

Acknowledgments

I would like to thank first a number of women who helped me with my work on this book. My initial study was published by the Harvard Women's Law Journal when other law reviews felt that the topic "would not be of interest to their readership." The editors and staff offered many suggestions and careful editorial review which clarified and refined my argument and analysis. I was also aided at this stage by many stimulating and fruitful discussions with my friend, Mary Bryan, an American law specialist.

I am grateful to my students and colleagues at the University of South Carolina for their help with my research and editing. I am particularly indebted to Brenda Baskin, an undergraduate student, who voluntarily contributed her excellent research capabilities and great enthusiasm, assisting me with all aspects of my work. Leann Brown, a graduate research assistant, came to help me through the support of the Department of Government and International Studies and the Institute of International Studies. Elna Corwin provided careful and patient assistance in putting much of the text of this work into the computer. The resources of the International Documents section of the Wilson Library of the University of North Carolina were invaluable, particularly the help of Librarian Pat Langelier. My departmental colleagues--Jan Love, Anne Sloan, Marsha Whicker and Ann Bowman--were an important source of continuing support as were my special friends--Jan Millsapps, Judy Jennings, Nancy Posselt, Mary Beth Love, Betty Mandell, Carolyn Matalene, and Robyn Newkumet.

I especially want to thank the female members of my family: my sister, Susan Kaufman, who will understand all the reasons I have dedicated this book to her; my sister, Helene Kaufman, who first made me aware of the Women's Movement and who has inspired me with the excellence of her own work; my mother, Helen Carroll Kaufman, who has lived through and fortunately past a time when she had to

give up so much of herself for her children; and my
daughter, Carrollee Hevener, who has encouraged me just
by being her beautiful self and by sharing me so
patiently with my work.

I would also like to thank the men who have made
valuable contributions to my work. Peter Sederberg, Moss
Blachman, Paul Kattenburg, and Morse Peckham, my
colleagues at the University of South Carolina, have all
shared their challenging and critical ideas with me. I
also appreciate the encouragement of my two departmental
chairmen, Charles Kegley and James Kuhlman, who provided
financial and professional support for my research.
Thanks also Mahmoud Karem, for his help in obtaining many
of the United Nations documents which were essential to
my work. I greatly appreciate the consistent support of
my father, Manuel Kaufman, and my brother, Ted Kaufman,
who have always encouraged my various endeavors.
Finally, my special thanks to my friend and colleague,
David Whiteman, for his patient help and instruction in
the intricacies of word processing and his valuable
insights and thoughtful critique of the manuscript.

Natalie Kaufman Hevener

PART I

Introduction

Since 1945 more than twenty different international legal instruments have been drafted which deal specifically with women. Each of these documents reflects an international consensus on particular problems in the treatment of women and, as such, provide a unique insight into the state of international consensus on the role of women in society. The content of these instruments has been elaborately formulated, normally after prolonged and difficult negotiations under the auspices of the United Nations or one of its specialized agencies. The treaties have been, for the most part, widely ratified (see Summary Table) and are legally binding. Given the caution and seriousness with which governments enter into legal arrangements, these documents constitute a valuable subject of study as statements of international agreement, apart from the interesting but separate question of their domestic implementation.

The purpose of this volume is threefold: to make available this group of international legal documents which have in some way treated women as an identifiably separate group; to analyze the implicit assumptions made within the documents about the role of women in society; and to identify some basic patterns which have emerged in this process of codification. The number of treaties alone is striking given the subject matter. The conclusion of international agreements regarding women, as might be expected, has been particularly difficult to achieve for two reasons. First, states have traditionally been reluctant to discuss, let alone codify, those issues which they have viewed as essentially subject to domestic jurisdiction, and for most states any issue affecting the status of women would automatically be so defined.[1] Second, there is as yet no

----

[1] An excellent example of this reluctance is the history

consensus at the domestic level on what action would be
prove most effective for advancing the position of women.
Even where agreement exists among women, access to what
are predominately male channels for achieving such a
consensus within the community at large has typically
been severely limited.

The basic approach taken in assessing these
conventions is to develop three analytic categories and
to apply them to the provisions of the treaties. The
categories are used to organize the contents of the
documents according to the status of women they seek to
establish or maintain.[2] The categories are: protective,
corrective, and non-discriminatory.[3] Each category
contains different assumptions about women and each
reflects a different conceptualization of what
constitutes a desirable, fair, and ultimately just status
for women in society. The application of these
categories to the treaty provisions enables one to
identify: 1) the general thrust of the treaty if its
provisions fall predominately into one category; 2)
ambiguous or even conflicting goals within a single
treaty if provisions fall into more than one category;
and 3) historical patterns of international consensus if
provisions of several conventions during a given time
period fall within a single category.

----

of United Nations efforts and failure to forge an
international consensus on population problems. The
world community has, however, made progress in areas
once considered to fall within domestic jurisdiction;
early opposition to review of colonial policies was set
in this framework and has persisted to the present
(Namibia). Issues remaining today as obvious examples
of domestic jurisdiction claims include: nationality
(and statelessness), immigration policies, human
rights, air and water pollution, high seas and economic
zones.

[2] For a descriptive treatment of international agreements
concerning the status of women concluded by or under
the auspices of the United Nations, see McDougal,
Lasswell, and Chen. "Human Rights for Women and World
Public Order: The Outlawing of Sex-Based
Discrimination." American Journal of International Law
69, no. 3 (July, 1975).pp.497-553.

[3] These categories are my own. They were first developed
in N.K.Hevener. "International Law and the Status of
Women: An Analysis of International Legal Instruments

The protective category describes those provisions which reflect a societal conceptualization of women as a group which either should not or cannot engage in specified activities. They imply that women are a subordinate group in society. The protection normally takes the form of exclusionary provisions, articles which stipulate certain activities from which women are prohibited. These provisions apply to all women, as a class. They do not apply to any men, and the protection afforded is of unlimited duration.

The corrective category also identifies women as a separate group which needs special treatment, but corrective provisions are significantly different from protective ones. The aim of the corrective provision is to alter and improve specific treatment that women are receiving, without making any overt comparison to the treatment of men in the area. The corrective provisions are inclusionary rather than exclusionary, often removing a previous bar to activity. They, too, refer to all women, as a class, and do not apply to men. They may be of limited duration, depending on the time period required to achieve the alteration desired.

Finally, the non-discriminatory, sex-neutral, category includes provisions which reject a conceptualization of women as a separate group, and rather reflect one of men and women as entitled to equal treatment. The concept is one which holds that biological differences should not be a basis for the social and political allocation of benefits and burdens within a society. These provisions treat women in the same manner as men. When women are specifically referred to as a class, it is only with the aim of ending existing separation or special treatment. The non-discriminatory documents, then, are inclusionary, since they seek to end discrimination against, or special treatment, of women. But, unlike the corrective documents, they apply to all men as well as to all women, with exceptions based on issue-related qualifications rather than sex-based distinctions. They are of unlimited duration.

The application of the categories to international conventions will be organized into three parts: 1) treaties of the 1945-1975 period; 2) recent non-treaty agreements; and 3) current international consensus, which reviews the 1979 Convention on the Elimination of All Forms of Discrimination Against Women which addresses in

----

Related to the Treatment of Women." Harvard Women's Law Journal 1, no.1 (Spring, 1978). pp.131-156. They represent an attempt to move beyond previous work which has been primarily descriptive and to provide systematic analysis of these international documents.

a single treaty many subjects found in the earlier documents. This study will identify the concept or concepts of women reflected in each of the various conventions and draw conclusions about the direction in which the treatment of women under international agreements is moving.

International Agreements, 1945-1972

The treaties discussed in this section were modified
or consummated between 1945 and 1975, the time between
the drafting of the United Nations Charter and the Mexico
City Conference which celebrated International women's
year and launched the United Nations Decade for Women.
For the most part the provisions of each of these
treaties tend to be consistent in the conceptualization
of women that it reflects and each can, therefore, be
associated with one of the three analytic categories.

Protective Conventions

The protective conventions identified herein deal
with specific economic issues and implicity accept the
traditional social definition of a woman as wife and
mother. Under the protective approach, the identity of
the woman who moves beyond the domestic sphere does not
alter, and she continues to be treated by the law with
regard to this primary role. The focus of legislative
attention is not on her actual activity but rather
remains on her domestic role, and it is the perceived
characteristics of this role that the law allegedly seeks
to protect. Thus, when the sphere of her actual work
involvement is viewed as being outside the normal domain
of women, her presence may be seen as necessitating
protection if her primary role is to be preserved.
Since under this view, women are usually treated as
subordinates when acting outside their traditional
domestic sphere, protective laws may openly authorize
permanent inferiority and thereby operate to maintain
this subordinate status. More common, however, and
equally damaging to women are those laws and legal
practices which codify an implied rather than a defined
inferiority. The view of women which such documents
project is analogous to that of children. Since women,
like children, are considered unable to make intelligent,

informed, and rational decisions about their own lives, they are subjected to the paternal power of the State, which seeks to protect them by completely proscribing or restricting their participation in certain areas of activity. For example, both of the protective conventions discussed below imply that the work concerned is undesirable for women with respect to time or place. If women are not allowed to perform the work, presumably it must be done by men. The intent would not appear to be consciously to deny positions to women because of a desire to increase opportunities for men, but rather to exclude women because of the stereotypic view that women could not or should not perform such work. In practice, however, so-called "protective" measures result in costly limitations of the number of options open to women by denying them the right to engage in certain activities and serve to perpetuate the presumption of their general legal incapacity to make independent judgements.

In addition, protective legislation, by fostering the social definition of women as essentially familial and as incapable of functioning with full responsibility outside the home, contributes both to women's reluctance to seek access to other domains of action and to the unwillingness of men to "allow" unrestricted opportunity once such action is taken. Protective measures, therefore, rather than discriminating in favor of women, ultimately discriminate against them.

Protective action at the international level has focused on the economic sphere, in which the protectionist objective is achieved by totally excluding women from two categories of employment: night work and mining. The original Convention Concerning Night Work of Women Employed in Industry was drafted in 1919 by the General Conference of the International Labour Organisation (ILO), and was revised and modified in 1934 and 1948. The most recent version sets forth a broad definition of industrial undertakings, defines "night," with some qualifications, as the hours between 10:00 PM and 7:00 AM and then states in Article 3:

> Women without distinction of age shall not be employed during the night in any public or private industrial undertaking, or in any branch thereof, other than an undertaking in which only members of the same family are employed.

The intent is clearly to protect women from the possible decision of working at a societally designated undersirable time. Having determined that it was undesirable for a woman to work at night, the drafters saw that the simplest way of insuring that this did not happen was to prohibit women from ever working at night, even if they should so desire.

The reasons for limiting the exclusion to the female sex might be based on assumptions such as that society has an interest in protecting the health, safety, and morality of women and in ensuring the welfare of the family unit. Men, on the other hand, presumably would not need protection, being stronger and healthier, not required to attend to the needs of their children, and perhaps more capable of making individual decisions as to their working hours based on the merits of the situation. Most likely, the decision included elements of each of these considerations. Interestingly, however, women's need of protection was not deemed to be absolute. Article 5 of the 1948 Convention reads:

> (1) The prohibition of night work for women may be suspended by the government, after consultation with the employers' and workers' organisations concerned, when in case of serious emergency the national interest demands it.[4]

A similar approach using a blanket prohibition was selected by the International Labour Organisation for the Convention Concerning the Employment of Women on Underground Work in Mines of All Kinds. Originally drafted in 1935 and revised in 1946, Article 1 of the Convention defines "mine" as including "any undertaking, whether public or private, for extraction of any substance from under the surface of the earth," and proclaims in Article 2:

> No female, whatever her age, shall be employed on underground work in any mine.

Again, the perception of the need to protect the woman's health for her role as wife and mother along with the notion of her physical incapacity were probably the bases for excluding her from mining, which is seen clearly as

----

4 As American scholars have observed with respect to night work laws in the United States, the willingness to cease worrying about women's various alleged incapacities for night work in times of national emergency allows for some skepticism about the "protective" assumptions and intentions of the drafters of this type of law. See, Night Work Laws, in B. Babcock, A. Freeman, E. Norton, and S. Ross, Sex Discrimination and the Law: Causes and Remedies (Boston: Little, Brown and Co., 1975).p. 470.

"man's work." Again, the conceptualization of women based on stereotypes which may be appropriate to women who do choose a domestic role or who are weaker physically results in excluding all women from a particular type of work. The reason men are not mentioned, again, is that it is simply assumed that men are suited to this type of labor and those men who are not physically or mentally equipped (as some women may be) are capable of making the individual judgment to refrain from work of this sort. In contrast to the sex-specific protective approach, non-discriminatory action in this area would acknowledge the undesirable aspects of mine or night work and require improved treatment or conditions for all workers regardless of sex. Thus, special standards for physical labor, travel time, etc., would be applied equally to men or women on the basis of specific requirements and appropriate qualifications, not on the basis of sex.

Corrective Conventions

The second category, corrective conventions, is based on the assumption that in some particular area women are not being treated fairly and that an effort to improve their treatment in that specific area needs to be made. There is no necessary reference to the treatment of men in the area, though there may be an implied minimum standard set by male treatment, the implication being either that men are not involved as victims (e.g., prostitution) or that men are not subject to the harmful practice under discussion (e.g., loss of nationality at time of marriage). Corrective legal action can usually be associated (by implicit secondary goals) with the protective or non-discriminatory type of action, but it primarily aims at righting a specific wrong.[5] Corrective legal activity may be examined as a meaningful indicator of societal treatment of women (what needs to be corrected) and it is important for improving the

----

5 We might note that preferential action, that is, action which is aimed at redressing past unfair treatment of women by temporarily giving them preference, might be placed in this category. Also, although it may clearly specify women for special consideration, it differs from protective action in two ways: 1) it is clearly temporary and 2) it has as its objective non-discrimination. It seeks to establish genuine equality before the law, something which solely non-discriminatory action does not achieve without a lengthy waiting period, if it achieves it at all.

treatment and general status of women. It can be helpful in areas of gross mistreatment and, because the scope of such agreements is specifically issue-oriented, such agreements may be relatively easier to conclude.

The earliest international effort with regard to corrective legal action deals with what is known as "the world's oldest profession." Beginning with an agreement in 1904, and extended through conventions in 1910, 1921, 1933, and 1947, the world community has attempted to regulate prostitution at an international level through prohibitions on the transporting of women and children for immoral purposes. Unlike domestic law in this sphere,[6] criminal culpability was laid directly on those who dealt in women for sexual purposes, rather than on the women themselves. The spirit of this regulation was protective but the object was corrective: the implicit assumption was that men were not victims of such activity and that they, therefore, did not need to be included in the treaty's terms. Article 1 of the International Convention for the Suppression of the Traffic in Women of Full Age clearly states its purpose:

> Whoever, in order to gratify the passions of another person, has procured, enticed or led away even with her consent, a woman or girl of full age for immoral purposes to be carried out in another country, shall be punished, notwithstanding that the various acts constituting the offence may have been committed in different countries. (Emphasis mine).

The protective spirit is implied in the phrase "led away even with her consent." The assumption is that a female, even of full age, cannot be expected to protect herself. A related indicator of this conceptualization of women is the International Convention for the Suppression of Traffic in Women and Children. Here women are grouped with children, who, we may agree, are properly viewed by society as being incapable of taking care of their own interests. Children of both sexes are included in the terms of the treaty, but no reference is made to adult males. As was the case with protective conventions, it is probable that men were not included in the terms of the Convention either because they were not perceived to be victims of this particular form of exploitation or because it was assumed that they could take care of

----

[6] See, e.g., the materials on prostitution laws in the United States in Babcock, Freeman, Norton, and Ross, Discrimination, pp. 877-914.

themselves.

Another target of international corrective action is legislation concerning the nationality of married women. The 1957 Convention on the Nationality of Married Women refers, in its preamble, to the provision of the Universal Declaration of Human Rights adopted in 1948 by the General Assembly of the United Nations, which holds that "everyone has the right to a nationality" and that "no one shall be arbitrarily deprived of his nationality nor denied the right to change his nationality." The treaty approaches the implementation of these rights by considering the special problems which have arisen for women at the time of marriage, separation and divorce. The treaty does not refer to men since, as the preamble to the Convention implies, men are not normally adversely affected at these times by an alteration of their legal status.[7] The treaty provides that a woman's nationality shall not automatically be affected by a marriage or its dissolution and that any change in the nationality of a man shall not automatically affect that of his wife. The treaty came about in response to the recognition that a large number of women had lost their nationality at the time of marriage, frequently without gaining the nationality of their husband until after long waiting periods, if at all. In addition, many women lost the right to reacquire their former nationality if their marriage was later dissolved. Thus, the Convention was designed to correct this particular injustice.

An additional area of corrective action, similar to the one just discussed, was identified by the General Conference of the International Labour Organisation through an extension of both the 1926 Slavery Convention and the 1930 Forced Labour Convention, in the Supplementary Convention on the Abolition of Slavery, the Slave Trade, and Institutions and Practices Similar to Slavery (1956). Basically, the modification took the form of an added section entitled "Institutions and Practices Similar to Slavery," which provided that the defined institutions and practices would be designated as illegal by the States Parties to the treaty and that they would take steps to see that such practices were abolished or abandoned in their countries. Included in

----

[7] Indeed, the official United Nations commentary on the Convention explains that the aim of the drafters was to discredit the anachronistic doctrine of "the unity of the family" as traditionally "headed by the husband," in favor of the principle of equality between the sexes. United Nations. Convention on the Nationality of Married Women: Historical Background and Commentary, U.N. Doc. E/CN.6/389 (1962). pp. 34-39.

this list are debt bondage, serfdom, and exploited child labor. With regard to women, the Convention proscribes the treatment of women as an object of commerce or inheritance. Article 1, paragraph c, prohibits:

Any institution or practice whereby:

(i) A woman, without the right to refuse, is promised or given in marriage on payment of a consideration in money or in kind to her parents, guardian, family or any other person or group;

(ii) The husband of a woman, his family, or his clan, has the right to transfer her to another person for value received or otherwise; or

(iii) A woman on the death of her husband is liable to be inherited by another person.

This extension of the Slavery Convention to correct a practice which had reduced women to a status similar to slavery was a significant effort to improve the treatment of women. Again, this action occurs in an area in which men have not been victimized, and they, therefore, did not need to be included in these provisions.

Non-Discriminatory Conventions

The third category of international action with respect to women is termed non-discriminatory. The objective of legal actions which are non-discriminatory is to revise the legal system in such a way that sex will no longer be a basis for the allocation of benefits and burdens in society. The fundamental assumption of non-discriminatory revisions is that whatever differences exist between the sexes should not be made the basis for differential treatment. However, non-discriminatory conventions make no necessary assumptions that (a) there are no differences whatever between the sexes, or that (b) such differences ought to be eliminated, or that (c) cultural characteristics presently associated with the female sex should be eliminated from the society. Instead, the goal of achieving truly non-discriminatory legal treatment is to broaden the range of behavioral options open to both sexes regardless of their inherent or cultural differences. By moving beyond the restraining social definition of women, non-discriminatory, sex-neutral, legal action attempts to create a climate in which both men and women have full access to all channels of fulfillment within the society.

One common form of non-discriminatory international legal action is contained in$_8$ general multi-lateral conventions and declarations. Although removing sex-based discrimination in particular was not a major concern in the drafting of these general anti-discrimination treaties, the provisions forbidding such actions are progressive, enlightened, and generally in advance of the national constitutions and statutes of the signatory states. Women are well aware of the chasm between de jure and de facto discrimination, but these treaties are one important step both in building the consensus necessary for future acton and legitimizing and providing incentive to national movements for non-discriminatory legislation and any necessary constitutional amendments.

The earliest major general convention endorsing the principle that sex shall be an impermissible basis for discrimination of any kind is the United Nations Charter. The Preamble to the Charter directly affirms "faith in . . . the equal rights of men and women," and Article 1 of the Purposes and Principles of the Organization includes the promotion of respect for human rights and fundamental freedoms "for all without distinction as to race, sex, language, or religion;. . ." (Emphasis mine).^{9} Other references to the non-discriminatory theme appear in Articles 13(1)(b), 55(c), 56, 62(2) and 76(c) of the Charter, in which members of the Organization pledge to take separate and cooperative action to promote universal respect for the human rights and fundamental freedoms of all without regard to sex or other distinctions.

The Universal Declaration of Human Rights, adopted by the General Assembly in 1948, employs similar language in Article 2:

----

8 They include the United Nations Charter, the Universal Declaration of Human Rights, the International Covenant on Civil and Political Rights, and the International Covenant on Economic, Social and Cultural Rights.

9 U.N. CHARTER, Art. 1, para. 3. For a Report on United Nations actions on issues of women's rights and treatment, see generally, Commission on the Status of Women, International Instruments and National Standards Relating to the Status of Women: Study of Provisions in Existing Conventions that Relate to the Status of Women, U.N. Doc. E/CN. 6/552 U.N.Document E/CN.6/552 (1972). See also, United Nations, The United Nations and the Advancement of Women: Study prepared by Mrs. M.K. Baxter, U.N. Document A/CONF. 32/L.7 (1968).

Everyone is entitled to all the rights and freedoms set forth in this Declaration, without distinction of any kind, such as race, colour, <u>sex</u>, language, religion, political or other opinion, national or social origin, property, birth or other status. (Emphasis mine).

The completely non-discriminatory nature of this document is evident in its treatment of the marriage issue, which may be compared to the corrective convention on this topic, as well as to the Civil and Political Rights Covenant discussed below. Article 16 of the Universal Declaration reads:

(1) Men and women of full age, without any limitation due to race, nationality or religion, have the right to marry and to found a family. They are entitled to equal rights as to marriage, during marriage and at its dissolution.

(2) Marriage shall be entered into only with the free and full consent of the intending spouses.

Even in this progressive document, however, there is one protective element, Article 25, which reflects the persistence of the traditional view of women. It provides, in part:

(2) Motherhood and childhood are entitled to special care and assistance . .

The important aspect of this provision, however, is that the reference to mothers, rather than all females, may indicate a willingness to distinguish women as workers, voters, officeholders, spouses, and so on, from women as parents. Once such a distinction is made, it is at least possible to conceive of a framework in which parents of both sexes may be treated in a particular fashion because of society's concern with the family, and women and men in their other roles would not be affected by sexually defined parental stereotypes.

In an attempt to promote and increase the application of the provisions of the Universal Declaration of Human Rights, two covenants on human rights were drafted and opened for ratification in 1966. Both have now come into force, and both include references to the elimination of sex-based discrimination.

The International Covenant on Civil and Political Rights states in Article 2, paragraph 1:

Each State Party to the present Covenant undertakes to respect and to ensure to all individuals within its territory and subject to its jurisdiction the rights recognized in the present Covenant, without distinction of any kind, such as race, colour, <u>sex</u>, language, religion, political or other opinion, national or social origin, property, birth or other status. (Emphasis mine).

And Article 3 stipulates specifically:

The States Parties to the present Covenant undertake to ensure the equal rights of men and women to the enjoyment of all civil and political rights set forth in the present Covenant.

In the provisions for derogation of obligations in time of national emergency, a State is prohibited from discriminating "solely on the ground of race, colour, <u>sex</u>, language, religion or social origin." (Emphasis mine). Article 23 goes on to incorporate the non-discriminatory provisions on marriage and divorce contained in the Declaration, and Article 24 drops considerations of motherhood and refers only to treatment of minors, in which case the protection to be afforded is not to be based on "race, colour, <u>sex</u>, language, religion, national or social origin, property or birth, . . ." (Emphasis mine). Article 26, which provides for equal protection of the law, includes the same list of prohibited discriminations.

The International Covenant on Economic, Social and Cultural Rights follows the same format as the sister covenant just discussed. Article 2 contains similar guarantees of non-discrimination based on the same list of factors, including sex. Article 3 states:

The States Parties to the present Covenant undertake to ensure the equal right of men and women to the enjoyment of all economic, social and cultural rights set forth in the present Covenant.

Article 7, dealing with work conditions, provides for fair wages, safe working conditions, reasonable limits on working hours. It also provides in paragraph (c) for

equal opportunity for everyone to be promoted in his employment to an appropriate higher level, subject to no considerations other than those of seniority and competence."[10]

These provisions are subject to the general provision for non-discrimination based on sex, and they therefore constitute a strong directive in this area. One particular reference in this Article that is especially useful and represents an improvement over previous treaties is the pledge to afford

> Fair wages and equal remuneration for work of equal value without distinction of any kind, in particular women being guaranteed conditions of work not inferior to those enjoyed by men, with equal pay for equal work; . . .

Four specifically issue-oriented international conventions of a non-discriminatory nature have also emerged. The first, another product of the International Labour Organisation, is the Convention Concerning Equal Remuneration for Men and Women Workers for Work of Equal Value adopted in 1951, which is a contemporary response to the protective action of earlier days. Although it presumably sought to remedy the recognized fact that women generally were not earning equal pay for equal work, there was nothing in the convention itself, or in its preamble, to indicate that this was the case. The non-discriminatory tone of the entire document is reflected in the second paragraph of Article 1, where the phrase "equal remuneration for men and women workers for work of equal value" refers to rates of remuneration established without discrimination based on sex. Nowhere in the convention are special categories established for preferential or protective treatment based on sex. There is, in fact, a marked absence of corrective elements. There are no provisions for compensatory payments to women for prior inequality of wages and no provision for improved access for women to positions paying higher wages. Rather, the convention moves from the present inequality by calling for sex-neutral descriptions of positions and the allowing for differentials only if they do not correspond to sex.

The next document in this group, the 1953 Convention on the Political Rights of Women, is a response to the fact that in most countries, at one time, women were not allowed to vote or hold public office and were thereby precluded from participation in the very processes which determined the nature and scope of their rights. The very existence of this convention indicates its

----

[10] COVENANT ON ECONOMIC, SOCIAL AND CULTURAL RIGHTS, Article 7, para. c.

corrective intent. However, the wording of the treaty is egalitarian and refers throughout to the rights of women "on equal terms with men." The consistently stated objective of the agreement is to place women on equal footing with men with regard to the exercise of political power.

The preamble to the third issue-specific document, the 1962 Convention on the Consent to Marriage, Minimum Age for Marriage and Registration of Marriages, sets out a corrective purpose, but the Convention covers those customs and laws which might also have adversely affected men. In only one phrase are females singled out as the victims of a practice requiring correction and that in the preamble - " the betrothal of young girls before the age of puberty." Although the drafters may have had practices exploitive of women in mind, they opted to use non-sexual terminology. Even in the preamble, they refer to the desired abolition of "such customs, ancient laws and practices by ensuring, inter alia, complete freedom in the choice of a spouse, eliminating completely child marriages. . . ." (Emphasis mine). This particular document, however, reveals one of the potential weaknesses of a non-discriminatory approach to the problem of improving women's status. In the section requiring the setting of a minimum age for marriage (Article 2), no reference is made to the desirability of insisting on the same age for both partners, despite the fact that it is generally true that the age requirement for women is lower than that for men. A corrective provision would have specifically addressed this situation; a strong non-discriminatory provision would have required that the minimum age be set without reference to the sex of the parties.[11]

A fourth non-discriminatory convention which includes sex as one prohibited basis for differential treatment is the 1960 Convention Against Discrimination in Education, drafted by the United Nations Educational, Scientific and Cultural Organization. It refers to the Universal Declaration of Human Rights and, in its preamble, seeks to impose a national duty not only to eliminate discrimination but also "to promote equality of opportunity and treatment for all in education." Article 1 provides:

----

[11] However, General Assembly resolution 2018, supplementing this convention in 1965, recommends that the minimum age of marriage be at least fifteen years of age for both sexes. General Assembly resolution 2018, Official Records of the General Assembly, 1965, Supp. (No. 14) 36, U.N. Doc. A/6014 (1965).

- 17 -

For the purposes of this Convention, the term
"discrimination" includes any distinction,
exclusion, limitation or preference which,
being based on race, colour, sex, language,
religion, political or other opinion, national
or social origin, _ economic condition or birth,
has the purpose or effect of nullifying or
impairing equality of treatment in
education . . . . (Emphasis mine).

The objective of this document is clearly
non-discriminatory. It has certain weaknesses, however,
because it lacks corrective provisions for altering past
and existing discriminatory practices. In addition,
although sex was included in the list above, the
Convention reflects the fact that disagreement persists
about what actually constitutes sexual discrimination.
Thus, Article 2 immediately reaffirms one aspect of
traditional educational system by providing in paragraph
(a) for:

The establishment or maintenance of separate
educational systems or institutions for pupils
of the two sexes, if these systems or
institutions offer equivalent access to
education, provide a teaching staff with
qualifications of the same standard as well as
school premises and equipment of the same
quality, and afford the opportunity to take the
same or equivalent courses of study . . . .[12]

Mixed Conventions

The consistency of the provisions within each of the
foregoing treaties resulted in their classification in
one of the three categories of analysis. Sometimes,
however, the provisions of a single agreement fall into
more than one category. The system of categorization
presented here can be fruitfully applied to these mixed
conventions; the analysis reveals the very different
conceptualizations of women in society which may be

----

[12] The debate in the United States over "separate but
equal" sex-segregated education centers on the concern
that single sex educational institutions may serve to
perpetuate sexual stereotypes, to the social and
economic disadvantage of women. See the materials on
the issue in Babcock, Freeman, Norton, and Ross,
Discrimination pp. 990-1036.

projected within a single convention. This subsection examines two such international agreements which have received widespread approval.

One example of such a mixed convention is the codification of international law on maternity benefits. A consideration of this problem by the General Conference of the International Labour Organisation gave rise to the Maternity Protection Convention, originally drafted in 1919. It provides a number of important benefits for pregnant women and nursing mothers, regardless of marital status These include paid leave before and after childbirth (Articles 3 and 4), job protection during such leave (Article 6), and nursing on the job "at times prescribed by national laws or regulations (Article 5)." The compulsory postnatal leave was to be no less than six weeks (Article 3). This Convention was expanded and modified in 1946, and again in 1952, and was supplemented for some women by the maternity provisions in the Convention Concerning Conditions of Employment of Plantation Workers.

Clearly, the drafters foresaw no need to include men in the Convention's coverage, since men are not viewed as subjects of mistreatment in this area. However, contemporary suggestions that the rights of fathers might also be considered in connection with the period of late pregnancy and postpartum care are the result of new reflections on the status of women as well as an increased interest in and social acceptability of a revised role for the father. The protective element in these conventions is clear: the female is viewed as primarily a mother during this time, with her job considered as a secondary, markedly less significant factor.

The Convention as currently drawn, however, also contains corrective elements. Nursing time, crucial to a woman's maintenance of a capacity for nursing, is an area which only need apply to women. The Convention seeks to insure that a woman may continue to work and to nurse concurrently during the early phase of child rearing. A related corrective element is that which provides that a woman's job be made secure during the time that she is forced to be away to give birth to the child. Prior to this Convention, (and unfortunately subsequent to it as well), it had been quite normal in some places for women to be dismissed once they became pregnant, and the recognition of the unfairness of this practice and its correction was an important feature of this otherwise protective convention. Women's status was not directly addressed but may have been helped indirectly by the general recognition of the legitimacy of mothers working outside their home and a woman's right to return to a non-discriminatory convention would have treated maternity leave the same as any other leave granted for health reasons (and equally available to men), and would have provided for child care leave during the period of early infancy available to a parent of either sex. Certainly, there are no medical grounds to justify the average woman's staying away from work for six weeks after normal delivery. The length of this period implicitly derives from some notion of the need of parental care for an infant, and there is no reason why such a "benefit" should be available only to women.

A second convention which projects differing views of women is the 1958 Convention Concerning Discrimination in Respect of Employment and Occupation. It sets out a non-discriminatory objective yet retains a protective spirit and will most likely produce only protective results. Drafted by the General Conference of the International Labour Organisation, the group that drafted the earlier protective economic conventions excluding women from night work and mining, this Convention also adopts the lofty aims of the more general conventions which attempted to eliminate various forms of discrimination. In the Preamble, reference is made to the Universal Declaration of Human Rights, and it is asserted that

> . . . all human beings, irrespective of race, creed or <u>sex</u>, have the right to pursue both their material well-being and their spiritual development in conditions of freedom and dignity, of economic security and equal opportunity. . . (Emphasis mine).

The first article defines discrimination as:

> . . . any distinction, exclusion or preference made on the basis of race, colour, <u>sex</u>, religion, political opinion, national origin, which has the effect of nullifying or impairing equality of opportunity or treatment in employment or occupation;. . . (Emphasis mine).

A corrective element appears in Article 1, paragraph 3, providing that access to vocational education be included in the general definition of employment and education and in the provision that requires national governments to eliminate discrimination as part of the overall program established by the Convention. A further corrective element is the establishment of a national authority for the supervision of activities such as vocational training and placement services (Article 3, paragraph (c).

Following the non-discriminatory introduction, and the above corrective elements, however, are several protective provisions. Article 5, paragraph 1 of the Convention states:

Special measures of protection or assistance provided for in other Conventions or Recommendations adopted by the International Labour Conference shall not be deemed to be discrimination.

This unqualified provision endorses the protective measures discussed earlier and would maintain the associated disabilities imposed on women. In addition, paragraph 2 of Article 5 states:

Any Member may . . . determine that other special measures designed to meet the particular requirements of persons who, for reasons such as sex, age, disablement, family responsibilities or social or cultural status, are generally recognized to require special protection or assistance, shall not be deemed to be discrimination. (Emphasis mine).

The protection here consists of two forms. First, the reference to the "particular requirements" of women, the old, young and disabled perpetuates the assumption that they need protection because as a class they are unable to take care of themselves. Again, allocating burdens and benefits on the basis of class membership rather than specific categories of qualifications results in an inequity to class as well as nonclass members.

Secondly, women in their roles as wives and mothers are accorded a special social and cultural status and as such they are "generally recognized" to require special protection. As has been noted, it is precisely because their status and social role are generally recognized as requiring protection that legal action of a corrective and genuinely non-discriminatory nature is perceived to be so badly needed. Thus, this Convention is internally contradictory in that it prohibits discrimination on the basis of sex except when it is necessary to discriminate on the basis of sex. And the discrimination is compounded by the inclusion of the very type of discriminatory legal action which this Convention could have taken an important step in eliminating.

Recent Non-Treaty Action

Some of the most important contemporary
international documents on the status of women are not
treaties; several are related to International Women's
Year and the United Nations Decade for women. Four of
the most important non-treaty instruments are: the
Declaration on the Elimination of Discrimination Against
Women; the Declaration of Mexico; the World Plan of
Action; and the Programme of Action. The Declaration on
the Elimination of Discrimination Against Women was
unanimously adopted by the General Assembly, on November
7, 1967. The Delaration of Mexico and the World Plan are
products of the International Women's Year Meeting in
Mexico City in 1975; the Programme of Action was adopted
at the World Conference in Copenhagen in 1980. Since
these documents are not conventions, they do not have the
binding nature of a treaty. They contain essentially
non-discriminatory provisions, and have as their stated
objective equalizing the rights, obligations, and general
status of men and women domestically as well as
internationally. These documents, however, contain a
number of corrective provisions which single women out as
a group in need of special attention. For example, in
the Declaration of 1967, Article 3 stipulates:

> All appropriate measures shall be taken to
> educate public opinion and direct national
> aspirations towards the eradication of
> prejudice and the abolition of customary and
> all other practices which are based on the idea
> of the inferiority of women.

While child marriage, a practice phrased in
non-discriminatory language, is disavowed, Article 6,
paragraph 3, of the same instrument identifies young
girls as a particular group which has been unfairly
subjected to betrothal before puberty and states a need
for the elimination of this practice. Articles 7 and 8

refer respectively to the need to eliminate penal code provisions which discriminate against women and to take steps to combat all forms of traffic in women.

Nevertheless, in all other sections equality of women with men is the clearly stated aim. Even in an area strongly associated with women, that of family allowance, equality is the desired basis for treatment. Article 10, paragraph 1, provides that "measures shall be taken to ensure to women, married or unmarried, equal rights with men . . .," including the "right to receive family allowances on equal terms with men."

The same pattern of a mixed approach is seen in the 1975 Declaration of Mexico. It is basically a non-discriminatory document, focusing on the need for equality of men and women. Article 1 broadly stipulates:

> Equality between women and men means equality in their dignity and worth as human beings as well as equality in their rights, opportunities and responsibilities.

Most of the rights specified in the human rights covenants appear in the Declaration in a non-discriminatory form.

The Declaration of Mexico contains, in addition, a large number of substantive and far-reaching corrective provisions, reflecting the increased emphasis on integrating women into the development of their countries[13] and fostering a true equality of status. Some of the more innovative corrective provisions are reproduced below:

> Article 8. All means of communication and information as well as all cultural media should regard as a high priority their responsibility for helping to remove the attitudinal and cultural factors that still inhibit the development of women and for projecting in positive terms the value to society of the assumption by women of changing and expanding roles.

---

[13] The integration of women into the development of their country is a major theme of the International Women's Year and the United Nations Decade for Women (1976-1985). It is the primary concern of most of the Third World delegations to the Commission on the Status of Women and international meetings concerned with the status of women.

Article 9. Necessary resources should be made
available in order that women may be able to
participate in the political life of their
countries and of the international community
since their active participation in national
and world affairs at decision-making and other
levels in the political field is a prerequisite
of women's full exercise of equal rights as
well as of their further development, and of
the national well-being.

Parts of Articles 17, 20 and 21, respectively, also speak
to women's equal role in national development:

In order to integrate women into development,
States would undertake the necessary changes in
their economic and social politics. . . .

. . . It is important to formulate and
implement models of development that will
promote the participation and advancement of
women in all fields of work, provide them with
equal educational opportunities, and such
services as would facilitate housework.

. . . Governments, the United Nations, its
specialized agencies and other competent
regional and international organizations should
support projects designed to utilize the
maximum potential and to develop the
self-reliance of rural women.

Furthermore, a provision excluding men calls for women to
combine their efforts. This provision represents an
important innovation in the corrective method in that it
bypasses the traditionally male-dominated political
structure in favor of an appeal to women as a group to
organize for action on their own behalf. Article 28
reads:

Women all over the world should unite to
eliminate violations of human rights committed
against women and girls such as: rape,
prostitution, physical assault, mental cruelty,
child marriage, forced marriage and marriage as
a commerical transaction.

The World Plan of Action, like the two Declarations,
represents a well thought out effort to move towards an
international consensus that sex should no longer be the
basis for allocation of burdens and benefits in domestic
or international activities. It combines a general

non-discriminatory approach with provisions for corrective action in specific areas in order to give the growing consensus actual implementation. The Plan provides suggestions, options and guidelines for national and international action on a full range of issues affecting the integration of women into the social, economic and political lives of their nations and the world.

One of the most significant aspects of these latest non-discriminatory documents is the unprecedented extent to which they outline a new role for men as well as for women and signify a genuine effort to make available a wider range of options to both sexes. For example, Article 5 of the 1975 Declaration reads:

Women and men have equal rights and responsibilities in the family and in society. Equality between women and men should be guaranteed in the family, which is the basic unit of society and where human relations are nurtured. Men should participate more actively, creatively and responsibly in family life for its sound development in order to enable women to be more intensively involved in the activities of their communities and with a view of combining effectively home and work possibilities of both partners.

Many of these same issues are addressed in a non-discriminatory way in the Copenhagen Programme of Action. It was adopted by the 1980 World Conference held in Copenhagen, Denmark, to mark the midpoint in the United Nations Decade for Women. The purpose of the Conference and the Programme was to review and evaluate the progress which had been made towards the implementation of the World Plan and to create and recommend strategies for further movement toward the general goal of advancing the status of women.

The Programme contains recommendations for national and international, governmental and nongovernmental action. As in the World Plan special emphasis is placed on the interdependence of equality, development, and peace, the three goals of the decade, and the need to make progress on several fronts simultaneously. The Programme calls on the United Nations to make comparative statistical surveys related to women in work, and to review its own hiring and promotion of female personnel.

As with the World Plan there are corrective provisions, one set in particular aimed at rural women and the urban poor. Special action is recommended in employment, health, and education, the sub-themes of the conference. For example, Part II, Section III, paragraph 49 (c) reads:

Providing women from the most disadvantaged
sectors of the population with the ways and
means of increasing their access to
infrastructure, basic services, and appropriate
technology in order to alleviate the heavy
workload imposed by the basic requirements and
demands of their families and communities,
women should also be provided with
opportunities to gain new skills and with job
opportunities in the construction and
maintenance of the above-mentioned services, as
well as in other sectors. . ..

Also, special corrective measures are called for and
approved by paragraph 50.

Governments should, where appropriate, design
certain special transitional strategies and
establish, compensatory mechanisms aimed at
achieving equality of opportunity in education,
employment and health as a means of overcoming
existing inequalities in national
administration, the educational system,
employment, health services and the like, it
being clearly understood that the special
strategies are designed to correct imbalances
and discrimination and will be phased out when
such imbalances and discrimination no longer
exist.

The last phrase indicates clearly that these are
corrective measures, and as such are of a temporary
nature.
The Programme devotes more attention than earlier
documents to the effects and uses of the mass media. It
calls on governments and media directors to work to
eliminate negative images of women in news and
advertising. In addition to this general, yet passive
demand of the media in their treatment of women's issues,
it calls for active steps to be taken: training programs
to "sensitize media personnel at all levels"; special
campaigns to eliminate prejudice and traditional
practices harmful to women; and training programs to
enable women to make use of media to express their views
and positions. And combining the use of media with the
objective of altering the social roles of both sexes, the
Programme of Action states in paragraph 91:

In all fields of activity, the mass media
should become one of the basic means in society
of overcoming the contradiction in, on the one
hand, the presentaton of women as passive,

inferior beings having no social significance
and, on the other hand, an accurate picture of
their increasing role and contribution to
society at large. The mass media should also
recognize that both parents have equal duties
and responsibilities for the training and
education of their children and for household
duties. Governments, as communicators, in
preparing communications to or about their
countries should ensure that output will
reflect government commitment to status of
women's issues and concerns.

The Programme of Action clearly aims at
non-discriminatory objectives and suggests movement
towards those objectives with primarily
non-discriminatory action. It has, however, a very
healthy share of corrective measures, specific and
general, aimed at redressing past inequities and making
it possible for women to gain the education, means, and
access that will make their assumption of an equal place
in society a reality.

Current International Consensus

The Convention on the Elimination of All Forms of Discrimination Against Women was adopted by the United Nations General Assembly on December 18, 1979. This Convention is the first to address a full range of issues related to the role and position of women in society. New topics are included but many of the subjects are those treated in earlier instruments. some in an altered form. Because this instrument reflects the major current international concerns related to the role of women in society, it is interesting to compare the measures outlined in this treaty with that of the earlier ones, to see in what manner legal obligations have been altered or maintained. The ultimate objective, using the categories developed and applied above, is to determine from this new multi-lateral convention the present international consensus on the preferred status of women.

Protective Provisions

As has been explained earlier, protective action at the international level has focused on the economic sphere, in which the protectionist objective is achieved by totally excluding women from certain types of employment. Most of the provisions in this latest treaty replace protective with non-discriminatory language. There are no references to particular types or forms of employment from which women are excluded. In addition, protectionist language, which we have seen in earlier treaties which were otherwise corrective or non-discriminatory, is almost entirely absent from this convention. One exception, however, is paragraph 2 of Article 4:

Adoption by States Parties of special measures, including those measures contained in the present Convention, aimed at protecting

maternity   shall   not   be   considered
discriminatory.

The problem here is that "maternity" is not defined, so
that one is left uncertain as to what is being protected
and who is determining the content and need for the
"special measures." The possibility exists that all
women during their childbearing years might be classified
as in need of protection and therefore excluded from a
wide variety of activities assumed to be dangerous to
potential mothers. Certainly in the past, women have
frequently been accorded a special social and cultural
status and thereby designated as needing special
protection. It is precisely because of this historical
designation that legal action of a corrective or
non-discriminatory nature is so badly needed.
        Given the present distribution of political,
economic, and legal power within and among States, women
may find themselves the objects of special measures
(exclusions from certain jobs, enforced and lengthy
prenatal and postpartum leaves, etc.) imposed on them by
men who are so often in the position to make the relevant
interpretations of legal provisions. Because of Article
4, paragraph 2, such impositions would not be considered
as discriminatory under the terms of this treaty.[14]

Corrective Provisions

        Many of the corrective provisions of this convention
address problems which have provided the raison d'etre of
earlier treaties. The reference to these topics in this
treaty, however, does not make the previous documents
obsolete, but rather reemphasizes these issue areas and
draws attention to the continuing existence of the
original problems. For example, the presence in this
convention drafted in the 1970's, of two problems
addressed as early as 1904, should serve to remind States
----

[14] A recent decision of the South Carolina Supreme Court,
pending a hearing on the merits, allowed the
imposition of a three month "maternity-leave" on a
deputy-sheriff in a county police department. Her job
will not be held for her during this leave. Mary
B.DuTremble v. Frank Powell as Sheriff of Richland
County; the County of Richland and Richard Black as
County Administrator. (Opinion not yet published.)

of the need to ratify the prior treaties on these
long-standing problems. Article 6 of the convention
under discussion reads:

States Parties shall take all appropriate
measures, including legislation, to suppress
all forms of traffic in women and exploitation
of prostitution of women.

The dehumanizing practices referred to in this article
were addressed in the Convention for the Suppression of
Traffic in Persons and of the Exploitation of the
Prostitution of Others (1949).[15] In addition to formally
defining the practices falling within the agreements and
identifying them as illegal, it offers national and
international strategies for preventing violations and
apprehending violators.

Another article of the convention reflective of
earlier codification concerns is Article 9:

States Parties shall grant women equal rights
with men to acquire, change or retain their
nationality. They shall ensure in particular
that neither marriage to an alien nor change of
nationality by the husband during marriage
shall automatically change the nationality of
the wife, render her stateless or force upon
her the nationality of her husband.[16]

In 1957, the Convention on the Nationality of Married
Women was concluded to address the not uncommon problem
of involuntary loss or change of nationality of women at
the time of marriage or divorce. The treaty explicitly
defines the problem and identifies State obligations in
this area, including that of making available "specially
privileged naturalization procedures" to alien wives of

----

[15] This treaty consolidated four international
conventions: International Agreement for the
Suppression of the White Slave Traffic (1904) as
amended in 1948; International Convention for the
Suppression of the White Slave Traffic (1910) as
amended in 1948; International Convention for the
Suppression of the Traffic in Women and Children
(1921) as amended in 1947; and International
Convention for the Suppression in the Traffic in Women
of Full Age (1933) as amended in 1947.

[16] This right is also included in the Declaration on
Elimination of Discrimination Against Women in Article
5.

nationals.[17]

The corrective effect of Articles 6 and 9 is, of course, far more limited than that offered by the earlier treaties, since no specific corrective measures are recommended or required.

On the other hand, new corrective ground is broken in this treaty on issues not addressed in previous conventions. The most extensive of these is contained in Article 14 which deals with special problems of rural women. This article is in part the result of serious demands made by Third World women at the 1975 U.N. Mexico City Conference marking the celebration of International Women's Year. These concerns are not referred to in the Declaration on Elimination of Discrimination Against Women. Article 14 lists a corrective series of provisions which outline State obligations to amellorate conditions which may also affect men, but were viewed by the drafters as having an especially devastating impact on rural women. Paragraph 1 of this article directs the attention of States to the special róle played by those women in the "non-monetized sectors of the economy." Paragraph 2 then states that the parties are required to "take appropriate measures . . . to ensure women the right:"

(a) To participate in the elaboration and implementation of development planning at all levels;

(b) To have access to adequate health care facilities, including information, counselling and services in family planning;

(c) To benefit directly from social security programmes;

(d) To obtain all types of training and education, formal and non-formal, including that relating to functional literacy, as well as, inter alia, the benefit of all community and extension services, in order to increase their technical proficiency;

(e) To organize self-help groups and co-operatives in order to obtain equal access to economic opportunities through employment or self-employment;

----

[17] Convention on the Nationality of Married Women, Article 3.

(f) To participate in all community activities;

(g) To have access to agricultural credit and loans, marketing facilities, appropriate technology and equal treatment in land and agrarian reform as well as in land resettlement schemes;

(h) To enjoy adequate living conditions, particularly in relation to housing, sanitation, electricity and water supply, transport and communications.

Although other women (non-rural) suffer from problems related to their participation in the "non-monetized sector of the economy," the treaty does little to offer badly needed corrective action for them. Women's unpaid contributions to the economy have only recently become the subject of serious study as more women enter the workplace and the division of labor between men and women there and in the home must be redefined.[18]

Another new area of corrective action occurs in Article 10. Here the States agree "to take all appropriate measures" to eliminate discrimination in education including

(f) The reduction of female student drop-out rates and the organization of programmes for girls and women who have left school prematurely.

The 1962 Convention Against Discrimination in Education covers a full range of topics but does not mention this particular problem.[19]

Most corrective conventions of the past have dealt with specific topics of limited scope. They have attempted to draw attention to a special problem, of which women have been the victims, and to provide a possible solution to the difficulty in the form of altered treatment of women in that particular area. The topics of these treaties have, for the most part, been

----

[18] See in particular Kathleen Newland, Women, Men, and the Division of Labor (Washington, D.C.: Worldwatch Paper 37, 1980).

[19] This particular issue is also missing from the 1967 Declaration on Elimination of Discrimination Against Women, which treats the general issue of education in Article 9.

- 32 -

treated in this convention in a much briefer form, and the corrective language has been replaced with non-discriminatory provisions.

For example, the need for corrective action was identified in an extension of both the 1926 Slavery Convention and the 1930 Forced Labor Convention, in the Supplementary Convention on the Abolition of Slavery, The Slave Trade, and Institutions and Practices Similar to Slavery of 1956. As we have seen above, the modification took the form of an added section entitled "Institutions and Practices Similar to Slavery" which provided that the defined institutions and practies would be designated as illegal by the States Parties and that they would take steps to see that such practices were abolished or abandoned in their countries. Included in this list are debt bondage, serfdom, exploited child labor, and a number of marital practices in which women are treated as objects or property. This extension of the slavery convention, intended to correct a practice which had reduced women to a status similar to slavery was a significant effort to improve the treatment of women. The present treaty covers this problem with broad non-discriminatory language in Article 16, paragraph 1:

> States Parties shall take all appropriate measures to eliminate discrimination against women in all matters relating to marriage and family relations and in particular shall ensure, on a basis of equality of men and women:
>
> (a) The same right to enter into marriage;
>
> (b) The same right freely to choose a spouse and to enter into marriage only with their free and full consent.

Changes like this one could result in de-emphasis of the temporary measures so badly needed to redress imbalances and past discriminatory practices. One mitigating factor, of course, would be past or future ratifications of the earlier corrective treaties. A second method of offsetting this disadvantage would be through the vigilance of the Committee on the Elimination of Discrimination against Women established in Article 17 of the treaty.[20] It could in its proceedings stress those

----

[20] Eventually the Committee will be composed of twenty-three experts, serving in their personal capacity and representing the major legal systems, forms of civilizations, and geographic regions.

areas which in the past have provided evidence of sexual discrimination and continue efforts[21] exemplified by the Copenhagen Programme of Action.[21] Also the U.N. Commission on the Status of Women, which drafted this treaty, continues to make a vital contribution, through resolutions and other activities which focus attention on the areas of greatest need.

Furthermore, some of the possible disadvantages of casting problems in non-discriminatory rather than corrective language could be offset by a liberal use of Article 4, paragraph 1 of the treaty. It allows that:

> Adoption by States Parties of temporary special measures aimed at accelerating de facto equality between men and women shall not be considered discrimination as defined in the present Convention, but shall in no way entail as a consequence the maintenance of unequal or separate standards; these measures shall be discontinued when the objectives of equality of opportunity and treatment have been achieved.

It would, therefore, be legally acceptable and socially desirable, to implement many of the present convention articles through measures of the type defined in this article. Thus, the corrective steps outlined in earlier treaties, although not required, could be instituted under Article 4, paragraph 1.

Non-Discriminatory Provisions

The content of the Convention on the Elimination of All Forms of Discrmination Against Women is overwhelmingly non-discriminatory. The goal is clearly set forth as that of equality of women with men, and discrimination against women is defined in Article 1 as

---

Article 18 requires States Parties to submit reports to the Secretary-General "on the legislative, judicial, administrative or other measures which they have adopted" to implement the treaty. Articles 19 through 22 describe the election and duties of the Committee which include the right to make suggestions based on a consideration of the reports received from the States Parties.

[21] This plan was drafted to state the objectives and strategies for the second half of the U.N. Decade for Women. U.N. Document A/Conf.94/35.

. . .any distinction, exclusion or restriction
made on the basis of sex which has the effect
or purpose of impairing or nullifying the
recognition, enjoyment or exercise by women,
irrespective of their marital status , on a
basis of equality of men and women, of human
rights and fundamental freedoms in the
political, economic, social, cultural, civil or
any other field.

And in Article 3 the States agree to work for the
development and advancement of women in order to afford
them their rights "on a basis of equality with men."

In Article 2 the States "condemn" discrimination and
take on the responsibility to "pursue by all appropriate
means" policies aimed at ending discrimination against
women. Explicit reference is made to the need for
constitutional amendment or legislation (sub-paragraph
(a)),[22] including sanctions (sub-paragraph (b)), and for
expanding legal protection of women's rights through the
judicial system and other public institutions
(sub-paragraph (c)). States also obligate themselves to
take steps to eliminate discrimination by "any person,
organization or enterprise (sub-paragraph (e))" and to
work to change "customs and practices as well as statutes
(sub-paragraph (f))," specifically penal provisions
(sub-paragraph (g)), which discriminate agaist women.[23]

In the area of public life, the treaty retains the
non-discriminatory mode established in the 1952
Convention on the Political Rights of Women and reaffirms
the rights of women set forth there to vote, stand for
election, and hold public office, "on equal terms with
men." In Article 7 it expands the definition of this
right to include: participation in the formulation and
implementation of government policy (sub-paragraph (b)),
participation in nongovernmental organizations and
associations involved in the public and political
activities of the State (sub-paragraph (c)). In
addition, in Article 8, it calls on governments to
provide women on equal terms with men "the opportunity to
represent their Governments at the international level
and to participate in the work of international
organizations."

----

[22] A similar provision appears in Article 2 of the
Declaration on Elimination of Discrimination Against
Women.

[23] A similar provision appears as Article 7 in the
Declaration on Elimination of Discrimination Against
Women.

Although as has been discussed above, the nationality issue is presented in corrective terms in Article 9, a second paragraph which is non-discriminatory calls upon States to "grant women equal rights with men with respect to the nationality of their children." This right is not discussed in earlier treaties.

Also the issue of child marriage, although more frequently a problem with girls, is addressed in non-discriminatory language in Article 16, paragraph 2.

The betrothal and the marriage of a child shall have no legal effect, and all necessary action, including legislation, shall be taken to specify a minimum age for marriage and to make the registration of marriages in an official registry compulsory.

This paragraph addresses in a general way the issues covered more specifically in the Convention on Consent to Marriage, Minimum Age for Marriage and Registraion of Marriages. The treaty requires States to take legislative action to remedy all three of these problems.[24]

In Article 10, the States Parties obligate themselves to eliminate discrimination against women in the field of education. In non-discriminatory language, they cover a number of important concerns: access to career and vocational guidance at all levels: preschool, general, technical, professional, higher technical, and vocational (sub-paragraph (a)) and access to the same curricula, examinations, equally qualified teachers, and the same quality of school premises and equipment (sub-paragraph (b)). This article deals with the same subject as the Convention Against Discrimination in Education which covers a broad range of topics and is predominantly non-discriminatory. It, too, lacks the necessary corrective measures significantly absent from this earlier treaty, but these measures could be taken, of course, through the use of Article 4, paragraph 1. One interesting advance over the earlier treaty is represented in sub-paragraph (c) which refers to the desirability of coeducation. Article 2 of the earlier

----

[24] These issues are also addressed in Article 2 of the Supplementary Convention on the Abolition of Slavery, the Slave Trade, and Institutions and Practices Similar to Slavery, which covers prescription of suitable minimum age for marriage, encouragement of practices which would allow open expression of free consent to marriage and support for registration of marriages.

convention reaffirmed the acceptability of separation on the basis of sex by providing that:

(a) The establishment or maintenance of separate educational systems or institutions for pupils of the two sexes, if these systems or institutions offer equivalent access to education, provide a teaching staff with qualifications of the same standard as well as school premises and equipment of the same quality, and afford the opportunity to take the same or equivalent courses of study . . .

would not be considered discrimination. Sub-section (c), paragraph 1 of Article 10 of the present treaty aims at:

(c) The elimination of any stereotyped concept of the roles of men and women at all levels and in all forms of education by encouraging coeducation and other types of education which will help to achieve this aim. . ..

The corrective nature of paragraph (f) of this article was discussed above.

In Article 11, on employment, the approach also is essentially non-discriminatory. The States Parties obligate themselves in paragraph 1 to take steps to ensure the same rights on a basis of equality of men and women. These include: the right to work (sub-paragraph (a)); the right to the same opportunities for employment and the same criteria for selection (sub-paragraph (b)); the right to free choice of profession and employment, to promotion, job security, and to vocational training and retraining (sub-paragraph (c)).[25]

This general topic is treated in the 1958 Convention Concerning Discrimination in Respect of Employment and Occupation, which sets out a non-discriminatory objective yet retains a protective spirit.[26] The non-discriminatory

----

25 These rights are treated in a narrower fashion in Article 10, paragraph 1, sub-paragraph (a), of the Declaration on Elimination of Discrimination Against Women.

26 This spirit is manifested in part in Article 5, paragraph 2 which provides that "Any Member may. . .determine that other special measures designed to meet the particulr requirements of persons who, for reasons such as sex, age, disablement, family responsibilities or social or cultural status, are generally recognized to require special protection or

language of Article 11 is commendable; as in other areas corrective action is needed as well.

Article 11 also deals with issues codified in the Convention Concerning Equal Remuneration for Men and Women Workers for Work of Equal Value. As with the earlier treaty, the provision on this issue is non-discriminatory. States Parties agree to ensure:

> (d) The right to equal remuneration, including benefits, and to equal treatment in respect of work of equal value, as well as equality of treatment in the evaluation of the quality of work. . ..

A novel alteration appears in this article in a provision of paragraph 1. In prior documents reproduction is only addressed in connection with females; here we have a non-discriminatory approach. States agree to ensure:

> (f) The right to protection of health and safety in working conditions, including the safeguarding of the function of reproduction.

This language exemplifies an easy solution which can afford protection to women as potential mothers without treating women as a class and achieves the desirable end of protecting the reproductive capacity of all workers.

Further elaboration of the rights of women on an independent basis, unrelated to any male defining figure (father or husband), appears in Articles 13 and 15. Article 13 deals with other questions of economic and social life and affords on a basis of equality of men and women:

> (a) The right to family benefits;

> (b) The right to bank loans, mortgages and other forms of financial credit;

> (c) The right to participate in recreational activities, sports and all aspects of cultural life.

----

assistance, shall not be deemed to be discrimination." The reference to the "particular requirements" of women, the old, young, and disabled perpetuates the assumption that they need protection because as a class they are unable to take care of themselves.

These topics have all been mentioned in earlier documents but are codified for the first time here.[27]

Article 15 also establishes new legal duties for States in a more complete form than any previous document.

2. States Parties shall accord to women, in civil matters, a legal capacity identical to that of men and the same opportunities to exercise that capacity. In particular, they shall give women equal rights to conclude contracts and to administer property and shall treat them equally in all stages of procedure in courts and tribunals.

3. States Parties agree that all contracts and all other private instruments of any kind with a legal effect which is directed at restricting the legal capacity of women shall be deemed null and void.

4. States Parties shall accord to men and women the same rights with regard to the law relating to the movement of persons and the freedom to choose their residence and domicile.[28]

The Declaration on Elimination of Discrimination Against Women contains general wording which appropriately has been defined and specified in the process of codification. Since there are no specific treaties or treaty provisions which deal with this extremely important set of rights,[29] the Convention represents a very significant advance in the

----

[27] The reference to cultural life in sub-paragraph (c) is covered in Articles 3 and 15 of the Covenant on Economic, Social and Cultural Rights of 1966.

[28] The Declaration on Elimination of Discrimination Against Women refers to these issues: Article 6, paragraph 1, sub-paragraph (a) corresponds to paragraph 2 here and sub-paragraph (c) of that article corresponds to paragraph 4 here.

[29] The Covenant on Civil and Political Rights in Article 12 provides for freedom of movement and choice of residence and also prohibits discrimination on the basis of sex.

international recognition of the full equality of women.

Provisions on Reproduction

The most difficult problem in the development of the rights of women is the consideration of any area which is perceived to be related in some way to the reproductive function: capacity for pregnancy; pregnancy; prenatal; immediate postpartum activity; lactation; and infant care. As discussed above, early protective conventions were based on the conception of woman as wife and mother. The generally non-discriminatory nature of this treaty, however, is seen in the preamble which is, as usual, a valuable indicator of the spirit and intent of the document's drafters.[30]

> Bearing in mind the great contribution of women to the welfare of the family and to the development of society so far not fully recognized, the social significance of maternity and the role of both parents in the family and in the upbringing of children, and aware that the role of women in procreation should not be a basis for discrimination but that the upbringing of children requires a sharing of responsibility between men and women and society as a whole. . ..

This clause clarifies the joint responsibilities of men and women and the significance of maternity as a role, not an identifying characteristic of women. This separation continues a much needed trend to recognize the necessity of distinguishing women from "potential mothers" and treating women as mothers only when such treatment is absolutely essential: during pregnancy and lactation. This separation also allows for a consideration of 1) directly relevant protective measures, and 2) measures which are optional for the mother and which allow her to make her own choices based on her evaluation of her need for such protection.

A second element of the preamble emphasizes another important step in the advancement of the status of women: the recognition of the interdependence of the redefinition of both sex roles.

----

30 See the Vienna Convention on the Law of Treaties Article 3.

Aware that a change in the traditional role of men as well as the role of women in society and in the family is needed to achieve full equality between men and women . . .

The objective of the treaty is genuine equality between the sexes; to achieve it the traditional roles of both men and women must be examined, altered, and potentially expanded.

Fortunately both these ideas from the preamble have been incorporated into the body of the treaty as well. The text of Article 5 reads:

States Parties shall take all appropriate measures:

(a) To modify the social and cultural patterns of conduct of men and women with a view to achieving the elimination of prejudices and customary and all other practices which are based on the idea of the inferiority or the superiority of either of the sexes or on stereotyped roles for men and women;

(b) To ensure that family education includes a proper understanding of maternity as a social function and the recognition of the common responsibility of men and women in the upbringing and development of their children, it being understood that the interest of the children is the primordial consideration in all cases.

Although these ideas are mentioned in the Declaration on Elimination of Discrimination Against Women, Article 3, they have not been previously codified.

The most difficult area for women has been their entry into the workplace and the various forms of discrimination, overt and subtle, perpetrated in the guise of protection. Even the most recent documents have remnants of this tradition. Much of the remaining protective language on work in this convention is still an improvement in that it 1) limits the protection to pregnant women; 2) provides the opportunity to have the measures reviewed; and 3) offsets the broader possible interpretations and applications of protective provisions through additional provisions prohibiting the most damaging protective practices of the past. Some of these new provisions are corrective and some are non-discriminatory.

- 41 -

Corrective provisions, of course, have the advantage of highlighting the particular problem of extant discrimination and providing a remedy. Article 11, paragraph 2, begins with clearly corrective language in discussing past discrimination at the workplace.

In order to prevent discrimination against women on the grounds of marriage or maternity and to ensure their effective right to work, States Parties shall take appropriate measures:

(a) To prohibit, subject to the imposition of sanctions, dismissal on the grounds of pregnancy or of maternity leave and discrimination in dismissals on the basis of marital status;

(b) To introduce maternity leave with pay or with comparable social benefits without loss of former employment, seniority or social allowances.

These rights are covered in a more complete way in the Convention Concerning Maternity Protection adopted by the International Labour Organisation in 1952. It defines the exact period and conditions of maternity leave (Article 3) and prohibits job dismissal during such leave (Article 6). This treaty covers women in industrial undertakings, nonindustrial and agricultural occupations including wage earners who work at home, while a similar set of provisions is included in the 1958 Convention Concerning Conditions of Employment of Plantation Workers.[31]

Paragraph 3 affords an opportunity for review of any protective measures which may have become obsolete.

3. Protective legislation relating to matters covered in this article shall be reviewed periodically in the light of scientific and technological knowledge and shall be revised, repealed or extended as necessary.[32]

----

[31] These and the rights discussed later are found in Part VII, Articles 46 through 50.

[32] It is interesting to note an amendment offered by the United States representative to the Commission on the Status of Women when this paragraph was being discussed. It represents an effort to creatively transform a protective measure into a non-discriminatory one. "To ensure the health and

- 42 -

The non-discriminatory language of the treaty appears in the first paragraph of Article 11.

States Parties shall take all appropriate measures to eliminate discrimination against women in the field of employment in order to ensure, on a basis of equality of men and women, the same rights . . . .

In addition to the list of rights just discussed is the provision, already mentioned, which attempts to protect the function of reproduction (sub-paragraph (f)). Also, in sub-paragraph (c) of paragraph 2 of this article, when discussing social services connected to the workplace, particularly child-care facilities, the reference is to "parents" rather than to "mothers."

Although early treaties which dealt with women appear to have been primarily aimed at protecting them, later treaties emphasized efforts to <u>eliminate</u> a wide variety of unjust practices, or <u>correct them</u> through temporary assistance programs. <u>In all</u> three, the traditional female role of mother has received attention. In attempting to legitimize restrictions on women, on the grounds of their potential maternity, governmental representatives have been faced with overwhelming evidence that this function which they argue needs protection is itself not receiving appropriate minimum attention. With this awareness, plus the increased legitimation of social and economic rights,[33] an attitude has gained prominence which supports the remodeling of the initial protective argument narrowing its application and redirecting some of the responsibility into an active role for public service. Health care services are

----

safety of all workers, male and female, in their conditions of employment, States Parties which have enacted laws designed to protect women workers from hazardous conditions of employment shall undertake progressively to extend such protections to all workers." Commission on the Status of Women: Report on the Twenty-Sixth and Resumed Twenty-Sixth Sessions; E/5909 and E/CN.6/608, Supplement No. 3, paragraph 104, p.41.

[33] Since the drafting of the Universal Declaration of Human Rights, Articles 22 through 27, the completion of the Covenant on Economic, Social and Cultural Rights with 69 States Parties, and numerous U.N. resolutions, there has been a new status for economic and social rights and the need for governmental action to develop and implement them.

expanded to include family planning and special services during pregnancy and lactation. Thus Article 12 reads:

1. States Parties shall take all appropriate measures to eliminate discrimination against women in the field of health care in order to ensure, on a basis of equality of men and women, access to health care services, including those related to family planning.

2. Notwithstanding the provisions of paragraph 1 of this article, States Parties shall ensure to women appropriate services in connexion with pregnancy, confinement and the postnatal period, granting free services where necessary, as well as adequate nutrition during pregnancy and lactation.

Several of these norms are repeated in Article 14 which deals with rural women. Paragraph 1 is non-discriminatory providing that family planning information and services be available to both sexes. Paragraph 2, however, outlines corrective measures that need only apply to women.

As was mentioned above, a set of corrective measures in this area was codified in the Convention Concerning Maternity Protection. In addition to those already mentioned, provision is made in that treaty for pre- and postnatal medical benefits for doctor and hospital (Article 4) and nursing time at work (Article 5). Similar provisions are included in the Convention Concerning Conditions of Employment of Plantation Workers. The societal nature of these responsibilities is clearly seen in the requirement in both these treaties that the costs be paid by public funds or compulsory social insurance. Article 4, paragraph 8 of the 1952 treaty provides:

In no case shall the employer be individually liable for the cost of such benefits due to women employed by him.

Since these treaties outline more complete and specific corrective measures, they, too, need to be ratified.

The programs like those just described are a special exception in the corrective category, since they provide justification for a permanent ongoing special program for one sex; corrective action normally has an implied or explicit time period based on the expectation that discriminatory treatment of women in the area concerned will eventually be eliminated. One might argue, however, that these benefits are fundamentally non-discriminatory

- 44 -

in that the ultimate benefactors are male as well as female fetuses and infants.

In dealing with responsibility beyond the period of infancy, the treaty moves into actively non-discriminatory language. Article 16 which deals with marriage and family matters uses the same formula in its introductory statement of eliminating discrimination against women and ensuring them rights "on a basis of equality with men." It begins with the right to choose a spouse freely and to enter into marriage only with full consent. It then goes on to discuss parental rights and responsibilities in all matters relating to children: number and spacing of children (sub-paragraph (e)); access to information, education, and the "means to enable them to exercise these rights" (sub-paragraph (e)); guardianship, wardship, trusteeship and adoption of children (sub-paragraph (f)). As spouses, both men and women are identified as having the right to a profession, an occupation and , surprisingly, a family name (sub-paragraph (g)). And in an elaboration of the rights outlined in Article 13 both spouses are entitled to ownership, acquisition, management, administration, and disposition of property (sub-paragrah (h)). Many of the rights are, of course, already recognized for men, but this article recognizes them for women as well in the non-discriminatory language of equality.

Conclusion

This examination of the major international legal documents which concern the treatment of women has, through the application of three analytic categories, revealed strikingly different conceptualizations of the proper role of women in society. This analysis reveals the progressive trend towards using an increasingly non-discriminatory approach to the problems of women, supplemented by substantial use of necessary corrective provisions. Implicit conceptualizations of women's role in society have moved away from a restrictive definition of women as wife and mother only, reflected in earlier protective measures, towards in the most recent documents a more dynamic conceptualization of women's role. Continued effort to implement non-discriminatory and corrective provisions and to redraft outdated protective ones can increase the acceptance of this view of women domestically and internationally

The most recent statement on the preferred status of women, the Convention on the Elimination of All Forms of Discrimination Against Women, provides in a single document the current international consensus on a diverse set of topics. For the most part the treaty is non-discriminatory in its approach. Protective provisions have been almost entirely eliminated; women, at least under the terms of this convention, are no longer prohibited from certain activities purely on the grounds of sex. The major vestige of protection can be found in the treatment of maternity, and here the crucial defect is a failure to clearly define this term and set limits on its application. With regard to corrective provisions, the major advance is the clear legitimation of temporary programs to redress imbalances or eliminate wrongs which have developed due to previous discriminatory practices. Also, some of the previously corrective language has been translated in this treaty into non-discriminatory terms.

On the special and controversial topic of reproduction, the treaty is still predominantly non-discriminatory, affording protection to both sexes from work which may be harmful to the reproductive function, and emphasizing the joint rights and responsibilities of the parental role. It also retains from earlier treaties the recognition of some societal responsibility to provide publicly funded medical care and health services. It encourages an extended public service role in fostering the combination of work and family responsibilities through promotion of child care facilities and other related social services.

What emerges from a review of this treaty, and the set of legal documents preceeding it, is a critical process of redefining legitimate female activity beyond the traditionally limited roles of wife and mother. Provisions of these international legal documents reflect four stages of progress over time from 1) the treatment of all women as wives and potential mothers, and therefore, in need of protection at all times, to 2) recognition of the possibility of separating women in general from women temporarily identifiable as wives and mothers with only the latter in need of protection, to 3) the desirability of creating corrective measures for women who have been the victims of mistreatment in specific issue areas, and protective measures for women only in relation to maternity, to 4) the recognition of the role of men as well as women in the reproductive function and the need to protect both as potential parents and the desirability of creating supportive programs for women during pregnancy and lactation and for both parents during the child rearing years.

The next crucial step is the further development of strategies for the implementation of the rules and principles set forth in these treaties. First, every effort should be made to encourage States to ratify the Convention on the Elimination of All Forms of Discrimination Against Women. Since this treaty is a general one its non-discriminatory approach is desirable; however, some of the earlier measures from corrective conventions have not been included, which means that ratification of these conventions continues to be imperative. We have seen that these prior treaties, on the whole, provide a more elaborate definition of problems and more specialized and useful strategies for amellorating the undesirable conditions they address. Secondly, special attention should be focused on the World Plan of Action and the Copenhagen Programme of Action, two non-treaty instruments which are highly significant policy statements; the drafters of these documents avoided protective elements and moved assertively and with clear guidelines towards non-discriminatory goals through the use of corrective and non-discriminatory strategies of implementation. New treaties will be needed, however, in specific issue areas; such legal action will make obligatory the suggested actions of the Plan and Programme and aid in the implementation of the goals and programs they recommend. Thirdly, although a great deal can be done at the national level, regional and global intergovernmental and nongovernmental groups, have a continuing and essential role to play in stimulating and supporting national action as well as implementing within their agencies and programs the proposals and objectives presented in these instruments.

The corrective and non-discriminatory treaties and agreements, then, stand as progressive statements which can aid national as well as international efforts to advance the status of women. They clearly move beyond the traditional definition of a woman as wife and mother and reassert a broad set of rights for women in the home, at work, and in the public domain. They also reaffirm the desirability of broadening the potential roles of men as well as women, thereby fostering the development of a full range of options for both sexes.

PART II

1. Charter of the United Nations

Background

  The Charter of the United Nations was the first multilateral treaty which closly enunciated a norm of non-discrimination on the basis of sex. The Covenant of the League of Nations included articles which dealt with suppression of traffic in women and proper working conditions for all, regardless of sex. It also made provision for women to work at the League Secretariat, but unlike the Charter it did not directly deal with the general issue of sex discrimination. The Charter provisions also made possible the creation of the Commission on the Status of Women, established by the Economic and Social Council in June, 1946. The Commission, composed of fifteen members, has as its purpose the elimination of discrimination against women and the promotion of equality of women with men in all fields.[1]

----

[1] The Commission's reports can be found in United Nations publications normally with the indicator E/CN.6/. They are located with the Economic and Social Council Official Records. For a useful discussion of the work of the Commission see Margaret E. Galey, "Promoting Nondiscrimination Against Women: The UN Commission on the Status of Women." International Studies Quarterly 23, no.2 (June, 1979), pp.273-302.

Text (Excerpts)

Preamble

We the Peoples of the United Nations determined to save succeeding generations from the scourge of war, which twice in our life-time has brought untold sorrow to mankind,

to reaffirm faith in fundamental human rights, in the dignity and worth of the human person, in the equal righs of men and women and of nations large and small, and

to establish conditions under which justice and respect for the obligations arising from treaties and other sources of international law can be maintained, and

to promote social progress and better standards of life in larger freedom,

*   *   *   *   *

CHAPTER I

PURPOSES AND PRINCIPLES

Article 1

The Purposes of the United Nations are:

1. To maintain international peace and security, and to that end: to take effective collective measures for the prevention and removal of threats to the peace, and for the suppression of acts of aggression or other breaches of the peace, and to bring about by peaceful means, and in conformity with the principles of justice and international law, adjustment or settlement of international disputes or situations which might lead to a breach of the peace;

2. To develop friendly relations among nations based on respect for the principle of equal rights and self-determination of peoples, and to take other appropriate measures to strengthen universal peace;

3. To achieve international co-operation in solving international problems of an economic, social, cultural, or humanitarian character, and in promoting and encouraging respect for human rights and for fundamental freedoms for all without distinction as to race, sex, language, or religion; and

4. To be a center for harmonizing the actions of nations in the attainment of these common ends.

* * * * *

Article 13

1. The General Assembly shall initiate studies and make recommendations for the purpose of:

a. promoting international cooperation in the political field and encouraging the progressive development of international law and its codification;

b. promoting international cooperation in the economic, social, cultural, educational, and health fields, and assisting in the realization of human rights and fundamental freedoms for all without distinction as to race, sex language, or religion.

2. The further responsiblities, functions and powers of the General Assembly with respect to matters mentioned in paragraph 1(b) above are set forth in Chapters IX and X.

* * * * *

Article 55

With a view to the creation of conditions of stability and well-being which are necessary for peaceful and friendly relations among nations based on respect for the principle of equal rights and self-determination of peoples, the United Nations shall promote:

a. higher standards of living , full employment, and conditions of economic and social progress and development;

b. solutions of international economic, social, health, and related problems; and international cultural and educational cooperation; and

c. universal respect for, and observance of, human rights, and fundamental freedoms for all without distinction as to race, sex, language, or religion.

Article 56

All Members pledge themselves to take joint and separate action in cooperation with the Organization for the achievement of the purposes set forth in Article 55.

* * * * *

Article 62

1. The Economic and Social Council may make or initiate studies and reports with respect to international economic, social, cultural, educational, health, and related matters and may make recommendations with respect to any such matters to the General Assembly, to the Members of the United Nations, and to the specialized agencies concerned.

2. It may make recommendations for the purpose of promoting respect for, and observance of, human rights and fundamental freedoms for all.

3. It may prepare draft conventions for submission to the General Assembly, with respect to matters falling within its competence.

4. It may call, in accordance with the rules prescribed by the United Nations, international conferences on matters falling within its competence.

* * * * *

Article 76

The basic objectives of the trusteeship system, in accordance with the Purposes of the United Nations laid down in Article 1 of the present Charter, shall be:

a. to further international peace and security;

b. to promote the political, economic, social, and educational advancement of the inhabitants of the trust territories, and their progressive development towards self-government or independence as may be appropriate to the particular circumstances of each territory and its peoples and the freely expressed wishes of the peoples concerned, and as may be provided by the terms of each trusteeship agreement;

c. to encourage respect for human rights and fundamental freedoms for all without distinction as to race, sex, language, or religion, and to encourage recognition of the interdependence of the peoples of the world; and

d. to ensure equal treatment in social, economic, and commercial matters for all Members of the United Nations and their nationals, and also equal treatment for the latter in administration of justice, without prejudice to the attainment of the foregoing objectives and subject to the provisions of Article 80.

* * * * *

Table of Ratifications

Afghanistan	11/9/46	Bangladesh	9/17/74
Albania	12/14/55	Barbados	12/9/66
Algeria	10/8/62	Belgium	12/27/45
Angola	12/1/76	Belize	9/25/81
Antigua and		Benin	9/20/60
Barbuda	11/11/81	Bhutan	9/21/71
Argentina	9/24/45	Bolivia	11/14/45
Australia	11/1/45	Botswana	10/17/66
Austria	12/14/55	Brazil	9/21/45
Bahamas	9/18/73	Bulgaria	12/14/55
Bahrain	9/21/71	Burma	4/19/48

- 54 -

Burundi	9/18/62	Iraq	12/21/45
Byelorussian		Ireland	12/14/55
SSR	10/24/45	Israel	5/11/49
Canada	11/9/45	Italy	12/14/55
Cape Verde	9/16/75	Ivory Coast	9/20/60
Central African		Jamaica	9/18/62
Republic	9/20/60	Japan	12/18/56
Chad	9/20/60	Jordan	12/14/55
Chile	10/11/45	Kenya	12/16/63
China	9/28/45	Kuwait	5/14/63
Colombia	11/5/45	Lao People's	
Comoros	11/12/75	Democratic	
Congo	9/20/60	Republic	12/14/55
Costa Rica	11/2/45	Lebanon	10/17/45
Cuba	10/15/45	Lesotho	10/17/66
Cyprus	9/20/60	Liberia	10/15/45
Czechoslovakia	10/19/45	Libyan Arab	
Democratic		Jamahiriya	12/14/55
Kampuchea	12/14/55	Luxembourg	11/2/45
Democratic Yemen	12/14/67	Madagascar	9/20/60
Denmark	10/9/45	Malawi	12/1/64
Djibouti	9/20/77	Malaysia	9/17/57
Dominica	12/18/78	Maldives	9/21/65
Dominican		Mali	9/28/60
Republic	9/4/45	Malta	12/1/64
Ecuador	12/21/45	Mauritania	10/27/61
Egypt (U. A. R.)	10/22/45	Mauritius	4/24/68
El Salvador	9/26/45	Mexico	11/7/45
Ethiopia	11/13/45	Mongolia	10/27/61
Equatorial Guinea	11/12/68	Morocco	11/12/56
Fiji	10/13/70	Mozambique	9/16/75
Finland	12/14/55	Nepal	12/14/55
France	8/31/45	Netherlands	12/10/45
Gabon	9/20/60	New Zealand	9/19/45
Gambia	9/21/65	Nicaragua	9/6/45
German Democratic		Niger	9/20/60
Republic	9/18/73	Nigeria	10/7/60
Germany, Federal		Norway	11/27/45
Republic of	9/18/73	Oman	10/7/71
Ghana	3/8/57	Pakistan	9/30/47
Greece	10/25/45	Panama	11/13/45
Grenada	9/17/74	Papua New Guinea	10/10/75
Guatemala	11/21/45	Paraguay	10/12/45
Guinea	12/12/58	Peru	10/31/45
Guinea-Bissau	9/17/74	Philippines	10/11/45
Guyana	9/20/66	Poland	10/24/45
Haiti	9/27/45	Portugal	12/14/55
Honduras	12/17/45	Qatar	9/21/71
Hungary	12/14/55	Romania	12/14/55
Iceland	11/9/46	Rwanda	9/18/62
India	/10/30/45	Saint Lucia	9/18/79
Indonesia	9/28/50	Saint Vincent and	
Iran	10/16/45	the Grenadines	9/16/80

Samoa	12/15/76	Ukrainian SSR	10/24/45
Sao Tome and		Union of Soviet	
Principe	9/16/75	Socialist	
Saudi Arabia	10/18/45	Republics	10/24/45
Senegal	9/28/60	United Arab	
Seychelles	9/21/76	Emirates	12/9/71
Sierra Leone	9/27/61	United Kingdom of	
Singapore	9/21/65	Great Britain and	
Solomon Islands	9/19/78	Northern Ireland	10/20/45
Somalia	9/20/60	United Republic	
South Africa		of Cameroon	9/20/60
(Union of		United Republic	
South Africa)	11/7/45	of Tanzania	
Spain	12/14/55	Tanganyika	12/14/61
Sri Lanka	12/14/55	Zanzibar	12/16/63
Sudan	11/12/56	United States of	
Suriname	12/4/75	America	8/8/45
Swaziland	9/24/68	Upper Volta	9/20/60
Sweden	11/9/46	Uruguay	12/18/45
Syrian Arab		Vanuatu	9/15/81
Republic (Syria)	10/19/45	Venezuela	11/15/45
Thailand	12/15/46	Viet Nam	9/20/77
Togo	9/20/60	Yemen	9/30/47
Trinidad and		Yugoslavia	10/19/45
Tobago	9/18/62	Zaire	9/20/60
Tunisia	11/12/56	Zambia	12/1/64
Turkey	9/28/45	Zimbabwe	8/25/80
Uganda	10/25/62		

Source: United Nations, Multilateral Treaties Deposited with the Secretary-General: Status as at 31 December 1981 (New York: United Nations, 1982).

2. Convention Concerning the Employment of Women on Underground Work in Mines of All Kinds

Background

A Committee of the General Conference of the International Labour Organisation in June, 1934, on the basis of a report from the Director-General of the organization, recommended the drafting of a treaty prohibiting work by women in underground mines. The Conference approved the recommendation of the Committee and adopted the treaty at their next session on June 21, 1935. The treaty came into force on May 30, 1937, in accordance with Article 5, twelve months after the registration of two instruments of ratification.

The treaty prohibits all females, with the exception of those engaged in some special categories of work, from working in underground mines of all kinds. It also requires the application of its terms to colonial territories. In 1946 the International Labour Organisation adopted the Final Articles Revision Convention which made some formal alterations in response to the dissolution of the League of Nations. None of the substantive provisions of this treaty were changed but some formalities were altered in accord with the rules and titles provided for in the Final Articles Revision Convention.

Text

Preamble

The General Conference of the International Labour Organisation,

Having been convened at Geneva by the Governing Body of the International Labour Office, and having met in its Nineteenth Session on 4 June 1935, and

Having decided upon the adoption of certain proposals with regard to the employment of women on underground work in mines of all kinds, which is the second item on the agenda of the Session, and

Having determined that these proposals shall take the form of an international Convention,

adopts this twenty-first day of June of the year one thousand nine hundred and thirty-five the following Convention, which may be cited as the Underground Work (Women) Convention, 1935:

Article 1

For the purpose of this Convention, the term "mine" includes any undertaking, whether public or private, for the extraction of any substance from under the surface of the earth.

Article 2

No female, whatever her age, shall be employed on underground work in any mine.

Article 3

National laws or regulations may exempt from the above prohibition--

(a) females holding positions of management who do not perform manual work;

(b) females employed in health and welfare services;

(c) females who, in the course of their studies, spend a period of training in the underground parts of a mine; and

(d) any other females who may occasionally have to enter the underground parts of a mine for the purpose of a non-manual occupation.

Article 4

The formal ratifications of this Convention shall be communicated to the Director-General of the International Labour Office for registration.

Article 5

1. This Convention shall be binding only upon those Members of the International Labour Organisation whose ratifications have been registered with the Director-General.

2. It shall come into force twelve months after the date on which the ratifications of two Members have been registered with the Director-General.

3. Thereafter, this Convention shall come into force for any Member twelve months after the date on which its ratification has been registered.

Article 6

As soon as the ratifications of two Members of the International Labour Organisation have been registered, the Director-General of the International Labour Office shall so notify all the Members of the International Labour Organisation. He shall likewise notify them of the registration of ratifications which may be communicated subsequently by other Members of the Organisation.

Article 7

1. A Member which has ratified this Convention may denounce it after the expiration of ten years from the date on which the Convention first comes into force, by an act communicated to the Director-General of the International Labour Office for registration. Such denunciation shall not take effect until one year after the date on which it is registered.

2. Each Member which has ratified this Convention and which does not, within the year following the expiration of the period of ten years mentioned in the preceding paragraph, exercise the right of denunciation provided for in this Article, will be bound for another period of ten years and, thereafter, may denounce this Convention at the expiration of each period of ten years under the terms provided for in this Article.

Article 8

At the expiration of each period of ten years after the coming into force of this Convention, the Governing Body of the International Labour Office shall present to the General Conference a report on the working of this Convention and shall consider the desirability of placing on the agenda of the Conference the question of its revision in whole or in part.

Article 9

1. Should the Conference adopt a new Convention revising this Convention in whole or in part, then, unless the new Convention otherwise provides,

(a) the ratification by a Member of the new revising Convention shall _ipso jure_ involve the immediate denunciation of this Convention, notwithstanding the provisions of Article 7 above, if and when the new revising Convention shall have come into force;

(b) as from the date when the new revising Convention comes into force, this Convention shall cease to be open to ratification by the Members.

2. This Convention shall in any case remain in force in its actual form and content for those Members which have ratified it but have not ratified the revising Convention.

Article 10

The French and English texts of this Convention shall both be authentic.

The foregoing is the authentic text of the Underground Work (Women) Convention, 1935, as modified by the Final Articles Revision Convention, 1946.

The original text of the Convention was authenticated on 18 July 1935 by the signatures of F.H.P. Creswell, President of the Conference, and Harold Butler, director of the International Labour Office.

The Convention first came into force on 30 May 1937.

IN FAITH WHEREOF I have, in pursuance of the provisions of Article 6 of the Final Articles Revision Convention, 1946, authenticated with my signature this thirty-first day of August 1948 two original copies of the text of the Convention as modified.

Director-General of the International Labour Office:
Edward Phelan

Table of Ratifications

Afghanistan	5/14/37	Egypt (U. A. R.)	7/11/47
Angola	6/4/76	Fiji	4/19/74
Argentina	3/14/50	Finland	3/3/38
Australia	10/7/53	France	1/25/38
Austria	7/3/37	Gabon	6/13/61
Bahamas	5/25/76	German Democratic	
Bangladesh	6/22/72	Republic	8/20/75
Belgium	8/4/37	Germany, Federal	
Bolivia	11/15/73	Republic of	11/15/54
Brazil	9/22/38	Ghana	5/20/57
Bulgaria	12/29/49	Greece	5/30/36
Byelorussian		Guatemala	3/7/60
SSR	8/4/61	Guinea	12/12/66
Canada*	9/16/66	Guinea-Bissau	2/21/77
Chile	3/16/46	Guyana	6/8/66
China	12/2/36	Haiti	4/5/60
Costa Rica	3/22/60	Honduras	6/20/60
Cuba	4/14/36	Hungary	12/19/38
Cyprus	9/23/60	India	3/25/38
Czechoslovakia	6/12/50	Indonesia	6/12/50
Djibouti	8/3/78	Ireland	8/20/36
Dominican		Italy	10/22/52
Republic	8/12/57	Ivory Coast	5/5/61
Ecuador	7/6/54	Japan	6/11/56

- 61 -

Kenya	1/13/64	Swaziland	6/5/81
Lebanon	7/26/62	Sweden*	7/11/36
Lesotho	10/31/66	Switzerland	5/23/40
Luxembourg	3/3/58	Syrian Arab	
Malawi	3/22/65	Republic (Syria)	7/26/60
Malaysia	11/11/57	Tunisia	5/15/57
Mexico	2/21/38	Turkey	4/21/38
Morocco	9/20/56	Uganda	6/4/63
Netherlands	2/20/37	Ukrainian SSR	8/4/61
New Zealand	3/29/38	Union of Soviet	
Nicaragua	3/1/76	Socialist	
Nigeria	10/17/60	Republics	5/4/61
Pakistan	3/25/38	United Kingdom of	
Panama	2/16/59	Great Britain and	
Papua New Guinea	5/1/76	Northern Ireland	7/18/36
Peru	11/8/45	United Republic	
Poland	6/15/57	of Cameroon	9/3/62
Portugal	10/18/37	United Republic	
Saudi Arabia	6/15/78	of Tanzania	
Sierra Leone	6/13/61	Tanganyika	1/30/62
Singapore	10/25/65	Uruguay*	3/18/54
Somalia	11/18/60	Venezuela	11/20/44
South Africa		Viet Nam	6/6/53
(Union of		Yugoslavia	5/21/52
South Africa)	6/25/36	Zambia	12/2/64
Spain	6/24/58	Zimbabwe	6/6/80
Sri Lanka	12/20/50		

*Indicates the State has denounced the Convention.

Source: International Labour Office, List of Ratifications of Conventions: As at 31 December 1981 (Geneva: International Labour Office, 1982).

3. Universal Declaration of Human Rights

Background

The Declaration was prepared by the Commission on Human Rights. The Commission was set up by the Economic and Social Council and charged with the task of drafting an international bill of rights. The Commission prepared the Declaration as a first step in the process of establishing a set of internationally defined human rights. It was adopted by the General Assembly as Resolution 217 A (III) on December 10, 1948,by a vote of 48 to 0, with 8 abstentions.

The Declaration concentrates heavily on traditional Western civil and political rights, but includes several provisions relating to economic, social, and cultural matters. It is a resolution of the General Assembly and not a legally binding treaty, but many legal authorities refer to the Declaration as evidence of customary international law and as an important official elaboration of the general human rights provisions of the Charter.

Text (Excerpts)

Preamble

Whereas recognition of the inherent dignity and of the equal and inalienable rights of all members of the human family is the foundation of freedom, justice and peace in the world,

Whereas disregard and contempt for human rights have resulted in barbarous acts which have outraged the conscience of mankind, and the advent of a world in which human beings shall enjoy freedom of speech and belief and freedom from fear and want has been proclaimed as the highest aspiration of the common people,

Whereas it is essential, if man is not to be compelled to have recourse, as a last resort, to rebellion against tyranny and oppression, that human rights should be protected by the rule of law,

Whereas it is essential to promote the development of friendly relations between nations,

Whereas the peoples of the United Nations have in the Charter reaffirmed their faith in fundamental human rights, in the dignity and worth of the human person and in the equal rights of men and women and have determined to promote social progress and better standards of life in larger freedom,

Whereas Member States have pledged themselves to achieve, in co-operation with the United Nations, the promotion of universal respect for and observance of human rights and fundamental freedoms,

Whereas a common understanding of these rights and freedoms is of the greatest importance for the full realisation of this pledge,

Now, Therefore,

THE GENERAL ASSEMBLY

proclaims

THIS UNIVERSAL DECLARATION OF HUMAN RIGHTS as a common standard of achievement for all peoples and all nations, to the end that every individual and every organ of society, keeping this Declaration constantly in mind, shall strive by teaching and education to promote respect for these rights and freedoms and by progressive measures, national and international, to secure their universal and effective recognition and observance, both among the peoples of Member States themselves and among the peoples of territories under their jurisdiction.

Article 1

All human beings are born free and equal in dignity and rights. They are endowed with reason and conscience and should act towards one another in a spirit of brotherhood.

Article 2

Everyone is entitled to all the rights and freedoms set forth in this Declaration, without distinction of any kind, such as race, colour, sex, language, religion, political or other opinion, national or social origin, property, birth or other status.

Furthermore, no distinction shall be made on the basis of the political, jurisdictional or international status of the country or territory to which a person belongs, whether it be independent, trust, non-self-governing or under any other limitation of sovereignty.

*   *   *   *   *

Article 16

1. Men and women of full age, without any limitation due to race, nationality or religion, have the right to marry and to found a family. They are entitled to equal rights as to marriage, during marriage and at its dissolution.

2. Marriage shall be entered into only with the free and full consent of the intending spouses.

3. The family is the natural and fundamental group unit of society and is entitled to protection by society and the State.

*   *   *   *   *

Article 23

1. Everyone has the right to work, to free choice of employment, to just and favourable conditions of work and to protection against unemployment.

2. Everyone, without any discrimination, has the right to equal pay for equal work.

3. Everyone who works has the right to just and favourable remuneration ensuring for himself and his family an existence worthy of human dignity, and supplemented, if necessary, by other means of social protection.

4. Everyone has the right to form and to join trade unions for the protection of his interests.

* * * * *

Article 25

1. Everyone has the right to a standard of living adequate for the health and well-being of himself and of his family, including food, clothing, housing and medical care and necessary social services, and the right to security in the event of unemployment, sickness, disability, widowhood, old age or other lack of livelihood in circumstances beyond his control.

2. Motherhood and childhood are entitled to special care and assistance. All children, whether born in or out of wedlock, shall enjoy the same social protection.

* * * * *

4. Convention Concerning Night Work of Women Employed in Industry

<u>Background</u>

The original Night Work Convention was adopted by the General Conference of the International Labour Organisation in 1919. It came into force on June 13, 1921. In 1934 the General Conference requested a Conference Committee to consider possible revisions of the Convention. The first proposed revision concerned the exemption from the Convention's terms of women in higher posts. This issue had been considered at the Fifteenth session (1931) but had fallen short of the necessary two-thirds majority for adoption. At that point an advisory opinion of the Permanent Court of International Justice was requested which established that women in such posts did, in fact, fall under the treaty's terms. A new provision to exempt such women was adopted by the Committee. The second revision involved a redefinition of "night" to facilitate further ratifications by broadening the possible work hours to allow the running of a two shift workday. The Revised Convention, reflecting these two alterations, was adopted by the Conference by a vote of 121 to 1. The treaty came into force on November 2, 1936.

The need for a second revision of the Convention was raised during the regular process of ten year reporting on the Convention, established by the International Labour Organisation. The primary concern of those wanting revisions was the desire for an even more flexible definition of "night" than that established by the 1934 Convention. A Conference Committee considered suggestions and recommended a revision of the Convention. The 1948 revised Convention was adopted by the General Conference in June, 1948, by a vote of 120 to 2 with 9 abstentions. It came into force on February 27, 1951, in accordance with Article 14, twelve months after the registration of ratification by two Members.

The latest treaty redefines "night" to allow
employers greater flexibility. It provides for
suspension of the treaty's terms in cases of emergency
when the national interest would appear to justify it.
It also further broadens the exemption for women in
management positions that do not require manual labor.

Text

Preamble

The General Conference of the International Labour
Organisation,

Having been convened at San Francisco by the
Governing Body of the International Labour Office, and
having met in its Thirty-first Session on 17 June 1948,
and

Having decided upon the adoption of certain
proposals with regard to the partial revision of the
Night Work (Women) Convention, 1919, adopted by the
Conference at its First Session, and the Night Work
(Women) Convention (Revised), 1934, adopted by the
Conference at its Eighteenth Session, which is the ninth
item on the agenda of the session, and

Considering that these proposals must take the form
of an international Convention,

adopts this ninth day of July of the year one thousand
nine hundred and forty-eight the following Convention,
which may be cited as the Night Work (Women) Convention
(Revised), 1948:

PART I. GENERAL PROVISIONS

Article 1

1. For the purpose of this Convention, the term
"industrial undertaking" includes particularly--

   (a) mines, quarries, and other works for the
       extraction of minerals from the earth;

(b) undertakings in which articles are manufactured, altered, cleaned, repaired, ornamented, finished, adopted for sale, broken up or demolished, or in which materials are transformed, including undertakings engaged in shipbuilding or in the generation, transformation or transmission of electricity or motive power of any kind;

(c) undertakings engaged in building and civil engineering work, including constructional, repair, maintenance, alteration and demolition work.

2. The competent authority shall define the line of division which separates industry from agriculture, commerce and other nonindustrial occupations.

Article 2

For the purpose of this Convention the term "night" signifies a period of at least eleven consecutive hours, including an interval prescribed by the competent authority of at least seven consecutive hours falling between ten o'clock in the evening and seven o'clock in the morning; the competent authority may prescribe different intervals for different areas, industries, undertakings or branches of industries or undertakings, but shall consult the employers' and workers' organisations concerned before prescribing an interval beginning after eleven o'clock in the evening.

Article 3

Women without distinction of age shall not be employed during the night in any public or private industrial undertaking, or in any branch thereof, other than an undertaking in which only members of the same family are employed.

Article 4

Article 3 shall not apply--

(a) in cases of force majeure, when in any undertaking there occurs an interruption of work which it was impossible to foresee, and which is not of a recurring character;

(b) in cases where the work has to do with raw materials or materials in course of treatment which are subject to rapid deterioration when such night work is necessary to preserve the said materials from certain loss.

Article 5

1. The prohibition of night work for women may be suspended by the government, after consultation with the employers' and workers' organisations concerned, when in case of serious emergency the national interest demands it.

2. Such suspension shall be notified by the government concerned to the Director-General of the International Labour Office in its annual report on the application of the Convention.

Article 6

In industrial undertakings which are influenced by the seasons and in all cases where exceptional circumstances demand it, the night period may be reduced to ten hours on sixty days of the year.

Article 7

In countries where the climate renders work by day particularly trying, the night period may be shorter than that prescribed in the above Articles if compensatory rest is accorded during the day.

Article 8

This Convention does not apply to--

(a) women holding responsible positions of a managerial or technical character; and

(b) women employed in health and welfare services who are not ordinarily engaged in manual work.

PART II.   SPECIAL PROVISIONS FOR CERTAIN COUNTRIES

Article 9

In those countries where no government regulation as yet applies to the employment of women in industrial undertakings during the night, the term "night" may provisionally, and for a maximum period of three years, be declared by the government to signify a period of only ten hours, including an interval prescribed by the competent authority of at least seven consecutive hours falling between ten o'clock in the evening and seven o'clock in the morning.

Article 10

1.   The provisions of this Convention shall apply to India subject to the modifications set forth in this Article.

2.   The said provisions shall apply to all territories in respect of which the Indian legislature has jurisdiction to apply them.

3.   The term "industrial undertaking" shall include--

(a) factories as defined in the Indian Factories Act; and

(b) mines to which the Indian Mines Act applies.

Article 11

1. The provisions of this Convention shall apply to Pakistan subject to the modifications set forth in this Article.

2. The said provisions shall apply to all territories in respect of which the Pakistan legislature has jursidiction to apply them.

3. The term "industrial undertaking" shall include--

(a) factories as defined in the Factories Act;

(b) mines to which the Mines Act applies.

Article 12

1. The International Labour Conference may, at any session at which the matter is included in its agenda, adopt by a two-thirds majority draft amendments to any one or more of the preceding Articles of Part II of this Convention.

2. Any such draft amendment shall state the Member or Members to which it applies, and shall, within the period of one year, or, in exceptional circumstances, of eighteen months from the closing of the session of the Conference, be submitted by the Member or Members to which it applies to the authority or authorities within whose competence the matter lies, for the enactment of legislation or other action.

3. Each such Member will, if it obtains the consent of the authority or authorities within whose competence the matter lies, communicate the formal ratification of the amendment to the Director-General of the International Labour Office for registration.

4. Any such draft amendment shall take effect as an amendment to this Convention on ratification by the Member or Members to which it applies.

PART III. FINAL PROVISIONS

Article 13

The formal ratifications of this Convention shall be communicated to the Director-General of the International Labour Office for registration.

Article 14

1. This Convention shall be binding only upon those Members of the International Labour Organisation whose ratifications have been registered with the Director-General.

2. It shall come into force twelve months after the date on which the ratifications of two Members have been registered with the Director-General.

3. Thereafter, this Convention shall come into force for any Member twelve months after the date on which its ratification has been registered.

Article 15

1. A Member which has ratified this Convention may denounce it after the expiration of ten years from the date on which the Convention first comes into force, by an act communicated to the Director-General of the International Labour Office for registration. Such denunciation shall not take effect until one year after the date on which it is registered.

2. Each Member which has ratified this Convention and which does not, within the year following the expiration of the period of ten years mentioned in the preceding paragraph, exercise the right of denunciation provided for in this Article, will be bound for another period of ten years and, thereafter, may denounce this Convention at the expiration of each period of ten years under the terms provided for in this Article.

Article 16

1. The Director-General of the International Labour Office shall nofity all Members of the International Labour Organisation of the registration of all ratifications and denunciations communicated to him by the Members of the Organisation.

2. When notifying the Members of the Organisation of the registration of the second ratification communicated to him, the Director-General shall draw the attention of the Members of the Organisation to the date upon which the Convention will come into force.

Article 17

The Director-General of the International Labour Office shall communicate to the Secretary-General of the United Nations for registration in accordance with Article 102 of the Charter of the United Nations full particulars of all ratifications and acts of denunciation registered by him in accordance with the provisions of the preceding Articles.

Article 18

At the expiration of each period of ten years after the coming into force of this Convention, the Governing Body of the International Labour Office shall present to the General Conference a report on the working of this Convention and shall consider the desirability of placing on the agenda of the Conference the question of its revision in whole or in part.

Article 19

1. Should the Conference adopt a new Convention revising this Convention in whole or in part, then, unless the new Convention otherwise provides,

(a) the ratification by a Member of the new revising Convention shall *ipso jure* involve the immediate denunciation of this Convention, notwithstanding the provisions of Article 15 above, if and when the new revising Convention shall have come into force;

(b) as from the date when the new revising Convention comes into force this Convention shall cease to be open to ratification by the Members.

2. This Convention shall in any case remain in force in its actual form and content for those Members which have ratified it but have not ratified the revising Convention.

Article 20

The English and French versions of the text of this Convention are equally authoritative.

The foregoing is the authentic text of the Convention duly adopted by the General Conference of the International Labour Organisation during its Thirty-first Session which was held at San Francisco and declared closed the tenth day of July 1948.

IN FAITH WHEREOF we have appended our signatures this thirty-first day of August 1948.

The President of the Conference:
Justin Godart

The Director-General of the International Labour Office:
Edward Phelan

Tables of Ratifications

Night Work (Women) 1919

Afghanistan	6/12/39	Benin	12/12/60
Albania*	3/17/42	Brazil*	4/26/34
Angola	6/4/76	Bulgaria	2/14/22
Argentina	11/30/33	Burma	7/14/21
Austria	6/12/24	Burundi	3/11/63
Bangladesh	6/22/72	Central African	
Belgium*	7/12/24	Republic	10/27/60

Chad	11/10/60	Nicaragua	4/12/34
Chile*	10/8/31	Niger	2/27/61
Colombia	6/20/33	Pakistan	7/14/21
Congo*	11/10/60	Peru	11/8/45
Cuba	8/6/28	Portugal	5/10/32
Czechoslovakia*	8/24/21	Romania*	6/13/21
Democratic		Rwanda	9/18/62
Kampuchea	2/24/69	Senegal	11/4/60
France	5/14/25	South Africa	
Gabon	10/14/60	(Union of	
Greece	11/19/20	South Africa)*	11/1/21
Guinea	1/21/59	Spain	9/29/32
Guinea-Bissau	2/21/77	Sri Lanka*	10/8/51
Hungary*	4/19/28	Switzerland*	10/9/22
India	7/14/21	Togo	6/7/60
Ireland*	9/4/25	Tunisia*	5/15/57
Italy	4/10/23	United Kingdom of	
Ivory Coast	11/21/60	Great Britain	
Lao People's		and N. Ireland*	7/14/21
Democratic		United Republic	
Republic	1/23/64	of Cameroon*	6/7/60
Luxembourg	4/16/28	Upper Volta	11/21/60
Madagascar	11/1/60	Uruguay*	6/6/33
Mali	9/22/60	Venezuela*	7/3/33
Mauritania*	6/20/61	Viet Nam*	6/6/53
Morocco	6/13/56	Yugoslavia*	4/1/27
Netherlands*	9/4/22	Zaire	9/20/60

Night Work (Women) Convention, 1934

Afghanistan	6/12/39	Madagascar	11/1/60
Argentina	3/14/50	Mali	9/22/60
Belgium*	8/4/37	Mauritania*	6/20/61
Benin	12/12/60	Morocco	6/13/58
Brazil*	6/8/36	Netherlands*	12/9/35
Burma*	11/22/35	New Zealand*	3/29/38
Central African		Niger	2/27/61
Republic	10/27/60	Pakistan*	11/22/35
Chad	11/10/60	Peru	11/8/45
Congo*	11/10/60	Senegal*	11/4/60
Egypt (U. A. R.)*	7/11/47	South Africa	
France*	1/25/38	(Union of	
Gabon	10/14/60	South Africa)*	5/28/35
Greece*	5/13/36	Sri Lanka*	9/2/50
Guinea*	1/21/59	Suriname	6/15/78
Hungary*	12/18/36	Switzerland*	6/4/36
India*	11/22/35	Togo	6/7/60
Iraq*	3/28/38	United Kingdom of	
Ireland*	3/15/37	Great Britain	
Ivory Coast	11/21/60	and N.Ireland*	1/25/37

Upper Volta   11/21/60   Venezuela   11/20/44

Night Work (Women) Convention (Revised), 1948

Algeria	10/19/62	Jamahiriya	6/20/62
Angola	6/4/76	Luxembourg	3/3/58
Austria	10/5/50	Malawi	3/22/65
Bahrain	6/11/81	Malta	1/4/65
Bangladesh	6/22/72	Mauritania	11/8/63
Belgium	4/1/52	Netherlands*	10/22/54
Bolivia	11/15/73	New Zealand*	11/10/50
Brazil	4/25/57	Pakistan	2/14/51
Burundi	3/11/63	Panama	6/19/70
Comoros	10/23/78	Paraguay	3/21/66
Congo	6/4/71	Philippines	12/29/53
Costa Rica	6/2/60	Portugal	6/2/64
Cuba	4/29/52	Romania	5/28/57
Cyprus	10/8/65	Rwanda	9/18/62
Czechoslovakia	6/12/50	Saudi Arabia	6/15/78
Djibouti	8/3/78	Senegal	10/22/62
Dominican		South Africa	
Republic	9/22/53	(Union of	
Egypt (U. A. R.)	7/26/60	South Africa)	3/2/50
France	9/21/53	Spain	6/24/58
Ghana	7/2/59	Sri Lanka	3/31/66
Greece	4/27/59	Swaziland	6/5/81
Guatemala	2/13/52	Switzerland	6/5/50
Guinea	12/12/66	Syrian Arab	
Guinea-Bissau	2/21/77	Republic (Syria)	12/1/49
India	2/27/50	Tunisia	5/15/57
Iraq	11/17/67	United Republic	
Ireland	1/14/52	of Cameroon	5/25/70
Italy	10/22/52	Uruguay	3/18/54
Kenya	11/30/65	Viet Nam	10/26/65
Kuwait	9/21/61	Yugoslavia	6/20/56
Lebanon	7/26/62	Zaire	9/20/60
Libyan Arab		Zambia	2/22/65

*Indicates State has denounced the Convention.

Source: International   Labour   Office,   List   of
Ratifications of Conventions: As   at 31 December 1981
(Geneva: International Labour Office, 1982).

5. Convention for the Suppression of the Traffic in Persons and of the Exploitation of the Prostitution of Others

Background

This treaty consolidates four other conventions which were drafted to provide protection to women and children. The earliest of these is the International Agreement for the Suppression of the White Slave Traffic of May 18, 1904. This document was amended by the Protocol of December 3, 1948, adopted by the General Assembly of the United Nations. The second is the International Convention for the Suppression of White Slave Traffic of May 4, 1910, which was amended by the same protocol. The third is the International Convention for the Suppression of Traffic in Women and Children of September 30, 1921; it was amended by the Protocol adopted by the General Assembly of the United Nations on October 20, 1947. The fourth is the International Convention for the Suppression of Traffic in Women of Full Age, amended by the 1947 Protocol as well.

The Convention was drafted by the Third (Social, Cultural and Humanitarian) Committee of the United Nations and incorporated several modifications based on replies to questions submitted to the Sixth (Legal) Committee. The General Assembly debated the treaty in plenary session and adopted it in Resolution 317 (IV) of December 2, 1949, by a vote of 35 to 2, with 15 abstentions.

The treaty reflects the then dominant view within the Third Committee that prostitutes are victims and punishment should, therefore, fall on procurers. The treaty obligates States Parties to punish those who procure persons, even with their consent, for the purpose of satisfying another. Parties are also bound to punish those who exploit the prostitution of others. The treaty also covers those who are financially involved in the maintenance or running of a brothel or anyone who lets or rents premises for the purpose of the prostitution of others. The treaty extends to all colonies or trust territories of any State ratifying it. The Convention came into force on July 25, 1951, in accordance with Article 24, ninety days after the deposit of the second instrument of ratification.

Text

Preamble

Whereas prostitution and the accompanying evil of the traffic in persons for the purpose of prostitution are incompatible with the dignity and worth of the human person and endanger the welfare of the individual, the family and the community,

Whereas, with respect to the suppression of the traffic in woman and children, the following international instruments are in force:

1. International Agreement of 18 May 1904 for the Suppression of the White Slave Traffic, as amended by the Protocol approved by the General Assembly of the United Nations on 3 December 1948,

2. International Convention of 4 May 1910 for the Suppression of the White Slave Traffic, as amended by the above-mentioned Protocol,

3. International Convention of 30 September 1921 for the Suppression of the Traffic in Women and Children, as amended by the Protocol approved by the General Assembly of the United Nations on 20 October 1947,

4. International Convention of 11 October 1933 for the Suppression of the Traffic in Women of Full Age, as amended by the aforesaid Protocol,

Whereas the League of Nations in 1937 prepared a draft Convention extending the scope of the above mentioned instruments, and

Whereas developments since 1937 make feasible the conclusion of a convention consolidating the above-mentioned instruments and embodying the substance of the 1937 draft Convention as well as desirable alterations therein:

Now therefore

The Contracting Parties

Hereby agree as hereinafter provided:

Article 1

The Parties to the present Convention agree to punish any person who, to gratify the passions of another:

1. Procures, entices or leads away, for purposes of prostituion, another person, even with the consent of that person;

2. Exploits the prostitution of another person, even with the consent of that person.

Article 2

The Parties to the present Convention further agree to punish any person who:

1. Keeps or manages, or knowlingly finances or takes part in the financing of a brothel;

2. Knowingly lets or rents a building or other place or any part thereof for the purpose of the prostitution of others.

Article 3

To the extent permitted by domestic law, attempts to commit any of the offences referred to in articles 1 and 2, and acts preparatory to the commission thereof, shall also be punished.

Article 4

To the extent permitted by domestic law, intentional participation in the acts referred to in articles 1 and 2 above shall also be punishable.

To the extent permitted by domestic law, acts of participation shall be treated as separate offences whenever this is necessary to prevent impunity.

Article 5

In cases where injured persons are entitled under domestic law to be parties to proceedings in respect of any of the offences referred to in the present Convention, aliens shall be so entitled upon the same terms as nationals.

Article 6

Each Party to the present Convention agrees to take all the necessary measures to repeal or abolish any existing law, regulation or administrative provision by virtue of which persons who engage in or are suspected of engaging in prostitution are subject either to special registration or to possession of a special document or to any exceptional requirements for supervision or notification.

Article 7

Previous convictions pronounced in foreign States for offences referred to in the present Convention shall, to the extent permitted by domestic law, be taken into account for the purpose of:

1. Establishing recidivism;

2. Disqualifying the offender from the exercise of civil rights.

Article 8

The offences referred to in articles 1 and 2 of the present Convention shall be regarded as extraditable offences in any extradition treaty which has been or may hereafter be concluded between any of the Parties to this Convention.

The Parties to the present Convention which do not make extradition conditional on the existence of a treaty shall henceforward recognize the offences referred to in articles 1 and 2 of the present Convention as cases for extradition between themselves.

Extradition shall be granted in accordance with the law of the State to which the request is made.

Article 9

In States where the extradition of nationals is not permitted by law, nationals who have returned to their own State after the commission abroad of any of the offences referred to in articles 1 and 2 of the present Convention shall be prosecuted in and punished by the courts of their own State.

This provision shall not apply if, in a similar case between the Parties to the present Convention, the extradition of an alien cannot be granted.

Article 10

The provisions of article 9 shall not apply when the person charged with the offence has been tried in a foreign State and, if convicted, has served his sentence or had it remitted or reduced in conformity with the laws of that foreign State.

Article 11

Nothing in the present Convention shall be interpreted as determining the attitude of a Party towards the general question of the limits of criminal jurisdiction under international law.

Article 12

The present Convention does not affect the principle that the offences to which it refers shall in each State be defined, prosecuted and punished in conformity with its domestic law.

Article 13

The Parties to the present Convention shall be bound to execute letters of request relating to offences referred to in the Convention in accordance with their domestic law and practice.

The transmission of letters of request shall be effected:

1. By direct communication between the judicial authorities; or

2. By direct communication between the Ministers of Justice of the two States, or by direct communication from another competent authority of the State making the request to the Minister of Justice of the State to which the request is made; or

3. Through the diplomatic or consular representative of the State making the request in the State to which the request is made; this representative shall send the letters of request direct to the competent judicial authority or to the authority indicated by the Government of the State to which the request is made, and shall receive direct from such authority the papers constituting the execution of the letters of request.

In cases 1 and 3 a copy of the letters of request shall always be sent to the superior authority of the State to which application is made.

Unless otherwise agreed, the letters of request shall be drawn up in the language of the authority making the request, provided always that the State to which the request is made may require a translation in its own language, certified correct by the authority making the request.

Each Party to the present Convention shall notify to each of the other Parties to the Convention the method or methods of transmission mentioned above which it will recognize for the letters of request of the latter State.

Until such notification is made by a State, its existing procedure in regard to letters of request shall remain in force.

Execution of letters of request shall not give rise to a claim for reimbursement of charges or expenses of any nature whatever other than expenses of experts.

Nothing in the present article shall be construed as an undertaking on the part of the Parties to the present Convention to adopt in criminal matters any form or methods of proof contrary to their own domestic laws.

Article 14

Each Party to the present Convention shall establish or maintain a service charged with the co-ordination and centralization of the results of the investigation of offences referred to in the present Convention.

Such services should compile all information calculated to facilitate the prevention and punishment of the offences referred to in the present Convention and should be in close contact with the corresponding services in other States.

Article 15

To the extent permitted by domestic law and to the extent to which the authorities responsible for the services referred to in article 14 may judge desirable, they shall furnish to the authorities responsible for the corresponding services in other States the following information:

1. Particulars of any offence referred to in the present Convention or any attempt to commit such offence;

2. Particulars of any search for and any prosecution, arrest, conviction, refusal of admission or expulsion of persons guilty of any of the offences referred to in the present Convention, the movements of such persons and any other useful information with regard to them.

The information so furnished shall include descriptions of the offenders, their fingerprints, photographs, methods of operation, police records and records of conviction.

Article 16

The Parties to the present Convention agree to take or to encourage, through their public and private educational, health, social, economic and other related services, measures for the prevention of prostitution and for the rehabilitation and social adjustment of the victims of prostitution and of the offences referred to in the present Convention.

Article 17

The Parties to the present Convention undertake, in connexion with immigration and emigration, to adopt or maintain such measures as are required, in terms of their obligations under the present Convention, to check the traffic in persons of either sex for the purpose of prostitution.

In particular they undertake:

1. To make sure regulations as are necessary for the protection of immigrants or emigrants, and in particular, women and children, both at the place of arrival and departure and while en route;

2. To arrange for appropriate publicity warning the public of the dangers of the aforesaid traffic;

3. To take appropriate measures to ensure supervision of railway stations, airports, seaports and en route, and of other public places, in order to prevent international traffic in persons for the purpose of prostitution;

4. To take appropriate measures in order that the appropriate authorities be informed of the arrival of persons who appear, prima facie, to be the principals and accomplices in or victims of such traffic.

Article 18

The Parties to the present Convention undertake, in accordance with the conditions laid down by domestic law, to have declarations taken from aliens who are prostitutes, in order to establish their identity and civil status and to discover who has caused them to leave their State. The information obtained shall be communicated to the authorities of the State of origin of the said persons with a view to their eventual repatriation.

Article 19

The Parties to the present Convention undertake, in accordance with the conditions laid down by domestic law and without prejudice to the prosecution or other action for violations thereunder and so far as possible:

1. Pending the completion of arrangements for the repatriation of destitute victims of international traffic in persons for the purpose of prostitution, to make suitable provisions for their temporary care and maintenance;

2. To repatriate persons referred to in article 18 who desire to be repatriated or who may be claimed by persons exercising authority over them or whose expulsion is ordered in conformity with the law. Repatriation shall take place only after agreement is reached with the State of destination as to identify and nationality as well as to the place and date of arrival at frontiers. Each Party to the present Convention shall facilitate the passage of such persons through its territory.

Where the persons referred to in the preceding paragraph cannot themselves repay the cost of repatriation and have neither spouse, relatives nor guardian to pay for them, the cost of repatriation as far as the nearest frontier or port of embarkation or airport in the direction of the State of origin shall be borne by the State where they are in residence, and the cost of the remainder of the journey shall be borne by the State of origin.

Article 20

The Parties to the present Convention shall, if they have not already done so, take the necessary measures for the supervision of employment agencies in order to prevent persons seeking employment, in particular women and children, from being exposed to the danger of prostitution.

Article 21

The Parties to the present Convention shall communicate to the Secretary-General of the United Nations such laws and regulations as have already been promulgated in their States, and thereafter annually such laws and regulations as may be promulgated, relating to the subjects of the present Convention, as well as all measures taken by them concerning the application of the Convention. The information received shall be published periodically by the Secretary-General and sent to all Members of the United Nations and to non-member States to which the present Convention is officially communicated in accordance with article 23.

Article 22

If any dispute shall arise between the Parties to the present Convention relating to its interpretation or application and if such dispute cannot be settled by other means, the dispute shall, at the request of any one of the Parties to the dispute, be referred to the International Court of Justice.

Article 23

The present Convention shall be open for signature on behalf of any Member of the United Nations and also on behalf of any other State to which an invitation has been addressed by the Economic and Social Council.

The present Convention shall be ratified and the instruments of ratification shall be deposited with the Secretary-General of the United Nations.

The States mentioned in the first paragraph which have not signed the Convention may accede to it.

Accession shall be effected by deposit of an instrument of accession with the Secretary-General of the United Nations.

For the purposes of the present Convention the word "State" shall include all the colonies and Trust Territories of a State signatory or acceding to the Convention and all territories for which such State is internationally responsible.

Article 24

The present Convention shall come into force on the ninetieth day following the date of deposit of the second instrument of ratification or accession.

For each State ratifying or acceding to the Convention after the deposit of the second instrument of ratification or accession, the Convention shall enter into force ninety days after the deposit by such State of its instrument of ratification or accession.

Article 25

After the expiration of five years from the entry into force of the present Convention, any Party to the Convention may denounce it by a written notification addressed to the Secretary-General of the United Nations.

Such denunciation shall take effect for the Party making it one year from the date upon which it is received by the Secretary-General of the United Nations.

Article 26

The Secretary-General of the United Nations shall inform all Members of the United Nations and non-member States referred to in article 23:

(a) Of signatures, ratifications and accessions received in accordance with article 23;

(b) Of the date on which the present Convention will come into force in accordance with article 24;

(c) Of denunciations received in accordance with article 25.

Article 27

Each Party to the present Convention undertakes to adopt, in accordance with its Constitution, the legislative or other measures necessary to ensure the application of the Convention.

Article 28

The provisions of the present Convention shall supersede in the relations between the Parties thereto the provisions of the international instruments referred to in sub-paragraphs 1, 2, 3 and 4 of the second paragraph of the Preamble, each of which shall be deemed to be terminated when all the Parties thereto shall have become Parties to the present Convention.

FINAL PROTOCOL

Nothing in the present Convention shall be deemed to prejudice any legislation which ensures, for the enforcement of the provisions for securing the suppression of the traffic in persons and of the exploitation of others for purposes of prostitution, stricter conditions than those provided by the present Convention.

The provisions of articles 23 to 26 inclusive of the Convention shall apply to the present Protocol.

Tables of Ratifications

Convention on Traffic in Persons

Albania*	11/6/58	Japan	5/1/58
Algeria*	10/31/63	Jordan	4/13/76
Argentina	11/15/57	Kuwait	11/20/68
Belgium	6/22/65	Lao People's	
Brazil	9/12/58	Democratic	
Bulgaria*	1/18/55	Republic*	4/14/78
Burma+	3/14/56	Liberia+	3/21/50
Byelorussian		Libyan Arab	
SSR*	8/24/56	Jamahiriya	12/3/56
Central African		Luxembourg+	10/9/50
Republic	9/29/81	Malawi*	10/13/65
Congo	8/25/77	Mali	12/23/64
Cuba	9/4/52	Mexico	2/21/56
Czechoslovakia	3/14/58	Morocco	8/17/73
Denmark+	2/12/51	Niger	6/10/77
Djibouti	3/21/79	Norway	1/23/52
Ecuador	4/3/79	Pakistan	7/11/52
Egypt (U. A. R.)	6/12/59	Philippines	9/19/52
Ethiopia*	9/10/81	Poland	6/2/52
Finland*	6/8/72	Republic of	
France*	11/19/60	Korea	2/13/62
German Democratic		Romania*	2/15/55
Republic*	7/16/74	Senegal	7/19/79
Guinea	4/26/62	Singapore	10/26/66
Haiti	8/26/53	South Africa	
Honduras+	4/13/54	(Union of	
Hungary*	9/29/55	South Africa)	10/10/51
India	1/9/53	Spain	6/18/62
Iran+	7/16/53	Sri Lanka	4/15/58
Iraq	9/22/55	Syrian Arab	
Israel	12/28/50	Republic (Syria)	6/12/59
Italy	1/18/80	Ukrainian SSR*	11/15/54

Union of Soviet		Upper Volta	8/27/62
Socialist		Venezuela	12/18/68
Republics*	8/11/54	Yugoslavia	4/26/51

Final Protocol

Albania	11/6/58	Luxembourg+	10/9/50
Argentina	12/1/60	Mexico	2/21/56
Belgium	6/22/65	Niger	6/10/77
Brazil	9/12/58	Norway	1/23/52
Bulgaria	1/18/55	Pakistan+	3/21/50
Burma+	3/14/56	Philippines	9/19/52
Byelorussian		Poland	6/2/52
SSR	8/24/56	Republic	
Cuba	9/4/52	of Korea	2/13/62
Czechoslovakia	3/14/58	Romania	2/15/55
Denmark+	2/12/51	South Africa	
Ecuador+	3/24/50	(Union of	
Egypt (U. A. R.)	6/12/59	South Africa)	10/10/51
Finland+	2/27/53	Spain	6/18/62
Guinea	4/26/62	Sri Lanka	8/7/58
Haiti	8/26/53	Syrian Arab	
Honduras+	4/13/54	Republic (Syria)	6/12/59
India	1/9/53	Ukrainian SSR	11/15/54
Iran+	7/16/53	Union of Soviet	
Israel	12/28/50	Socialist	
Japan	5/1/58	Republics	8/11/54
Kuwait	11/20/68	Venezuela	12/18/68
Liberia+	3/21/50	Yugoslavia	4/26/51
Libyan Arab			
Jamahiriya	12/3/56		

+Indicates signature only.

*Indicates reservation or declaration at time of signature or ratification.

Source: United Nations, Multilateral Treaties Deposited with the Secretary-General: Status as at 31 December 1981 (New York: United Nations, 1982).

6. International Convention for the Suppression of the Traffic in Women and Children

Article 1

The High Contracting Parties agree that, in the event of their not being already Parties to the Agreement of May 18, 1904, and not being already Parties to the Agreement of May 18, 1904, and the Convention of May 4, 1910, mentioned above, they will transmit, with the least possible delay, their ratifications of, or adhesions to, those instruments in the manner laid down therein.

Article 2

The High Contracting Parties agree to take all measures to discover and prosecute persons who are engaged in the traffic in children of both sexes and who commit offences within the meaning of Article 1 of the Convention of May 4, 1910.

Article 3

The High Contracting Parties agree to take the necessary steps to secure punishment of attempts to commit, and, within legal limits, of acts preparatory to the commission of the offences specified in Articles 1 and 2 of the Convention of May 4, 1910.

Article 4

The High Contracting Parties agree that, in cases where there are no extradition Conventions in force between them, they will take all measures within their power to extradite or provide for the extradition of persons accused or convicted of the offences specified in Articles 1 and 2 of the Convention of May 4, 1910.

Article 5

In paragraph B of the Final Protocol of the Convention of 1910, the words "twenty completed years of age" shall be replaced by the words "twenty-one completed years of age".

Article 6

The High Contracting Parties agree, in case they have not already taken legislative or administrative measures regarding licensing and supervision of employment agencies and offices, to prescribe such regulations as are required to ensure the protection of women and children seeking employment in another country.

Article 7

The High Contracting Parties undertake in connection with immigration and emigration to adopt such administrative and legislative measures as are required to check the traffic in women and children. In particular, they undertake to make such regulations as are required for the protection of women and children travelling on emigrant ships, not only at the points of departure and arrival, but also during the journey and to arrange for the exhibition, in railway stations and in ports, of notices warning women and children of the danger of the traffic and indicating the places where they can obtain accommodation and assistance.

Article 8

The present Convention, of which the French and the English texts are both authentic, shall bear this day's date, and shall be open for signature until March 31, 1922.

Article 9

The present Convention is subject to ratification. As from 1 January 1948 instruments of ratification shall be transmitted to the Secretary-General of the United Nations, who will notify the receipt of them to Members of the United Nations and to non-member States to which the Secretary General has communicated a copy of the Convention. The instruments of ratification shall be deposited in the archives of the Secretariat of the United Nations.

In order to comply with the provisions of Article 18 of the Covenant of the League of Nations, the Secretary-General will register the present Covention upon the deposit of the first ratification.

Article 10

Members of the United Nations may accede to the present Convention.

The same applies to non-member States to which the Economic and Social Council of the United Nations may decide officially to communicate the present Convention.

Accession will be notified to the Secretary-General of the United Nations, who will notify all Members of the United Nations and the non-member States to which the Secretary-General has communicated a copy of the Convention.

Article 11

The present Convention shall come into force in respect of each Party on the date of the deposit of its ratification or act of accession.

Article 12

The present Convention may be denounced by any State which is a Party thereto, on giving twelve months' notice of its intention to denounce.

Denunciation shall be effected by notification in writing addressed to the Secretary-General of the United Nations. Copies of such notification shall be transmitted forthwith by him to all Members of the United Nations and to non-member States to which the Secretary-General has communicated a copy of the Convention. The denunciation shall take effect one year after the date on which it was notified to the Secretary-General of the United Nations, and shall operate only in respect of the notifying Power.

Article 13

A special record shall be kept by the Secretary-General of the United Nations, showing which of the parties have signed, ratified, acceded to or denounced the present Convention. This record shall be open at all times to any Member of the United Nations or any non-member State to which the Secretary-General has communicated a copy of the Convention; it shall be published as often as possible, in accordance with the directions of the Economic and Social Council of the United Nations.

Tables of Ratifications

Convention on Traffic in Women and Children

Afghanistan	4/10/35	Austria	8/9/22
Albania	10/13/24	Bahamas	6/10/76
Australia	6/28/22	Belgium	6/15/22

Brazil	9/18/33	Mexico	5/10/32
Bulgaria	4/29/25	Monaco	7/18/31
Byelorussian		Netherlands	9/19/23
SSR	5/25/48	New Zealand	6/28/22
Canada	6/28/22	Nicaragua	12/12/35
Chile	1/15/29	Norway	8/16/22
China	2/24/26	Pakistan	11/12/47
Colombia	11/8/34	Poland	10/8/24
Cuba	5/7/23	Portugal	12/1/23
Cyprus	5/16/63	Romania	9/5/23
Czechoslovakia	9/29/23	Sierra Leone	3/13/62
Denmark	4/23/31	Singapore	6/7/66
Egypt	4/13/52	South Africa	
Estonia	2/28/30	(Union of	
Fiji	6/12/72	South Africa)	6/28/22
Finland	9/16/26	Spain	5/12/24
France	3/1/26	Sudan	6/1/32
GermanY	7/8/24	Sweden	6/9/25
Ghana	4/7/58	Switzerland	1/20/26
Greece	4/9/23	Thailand	7/13/22
Hungary	4/25/25	Trinidad and	
India	6/28/22	Tobago	4/11/66
Iran	3/28/33	Turkey	4/15/37
Iraq	5/15/25	Union of Soviet	
Ireland	5/18/34	Socialist	
Italy	6/30/24	Republics	12/18/47
Jamaica	3/24/67	United Kingdom of	
Japan	12/15/25	Great Britain and	
Lithuania	9/14/31	Northern Ireland	6/28/22
Luxembourg	12/31/29	Uruguay	10/21/24
Malta	3/24/67	Yugoslavia	5/2/29
Mauritius	7/18/69	Zambia	3/26/73

Convention as Amended by the Protocol of 1947

Afghanistan	11/12/47	German Democratic	
Albania	7/25/49	Republic	7/16/74
Algeria	10/31/63	Germany, Federal	
Australia	11/13/47	Republic of	5/29/73
Austria	6/7/50	Greece	4/5/60
Belgium	11/12/47	Hungary	2/2/50
Brazil	4/6/50	India	12/12/47
Burma	5/13/49	Ireland	7/19/61
Canada	11/24/47	Italy	1/5/49
China	11/12/47	Jamaica	3/16/65
Cuba	5/16/81	Lebanon	12/12/47
Czechoslovakia	11/12/47	Libyan Arab	
Denmark	11/21/49	Jamahiriya	2/17/59
Egypt (U. A. R.)	11/12/47	Luxembourg	3/14/55
Finland	1/6/49	Madagascar	2/18/63

Malawi	2/25/66	South Africa	
Malta	2/27/75	(Union of	
Mexico	11/12/47	South Africa)	11/12/47
Netherlands	3/7/49	Sweden	6/9/48
Nicaragua	4/24/50	Syrian Arab	
Norway	11/28/47	Republic	11/17/47
Pakistan	11/12/47	Turkey	11/12/47
Philippines	9/30/54	Union of Soviet	
Poland	12/21/50	Socialist	
Romania	11/2/50	Republics	12/18/47
Sierra Leone	8/13/62	Yugoslavia	11/12/47
Singapore	10/26/66		

Source: United Nations, _Multilateral Treaties Deposited with the Secretary-General: Status as at 31 December 1981 (New York. United Nations, 1982)._

7. International Convention for the Suppression of the Traffic in Women of Full Age

Article 1

Whoever, in order to gratify the passions of another person, has procured, enticed or led away even with her consent, a woman or girl of full age for immoral purposes to be carried out in another country, shall be punished, notwithstanding that the various acts constituting the offence may have been committed in different countries.

Attempted offences, and within the legal limits, acts preparatory to the offences in question, shall also be punishable.

For the purposes of the present Article, the term "country" includes the colonies and protectorates of the High Contracting Party concerned, as well as territories under his suzerainty and territories for which a mandate has been entrusted to him.

Article 2

The High Contracting Parties whose laws are at present inadequate to deal with the offences specified in the preceding Article agree to take the necessary steps to ensure that these offences shall be punished in accordance with their gravity.

Article 3

The High Contracting Parties undertake to communicate to each other in regard to any person of either sex who has committed or attempted to commit any of the offences referred to in the present Convention or in the Conventions of 1910 and 1921 on the Suppression of the Traffic in Women and Children, the various constituent acts of which were, or were to have been, accomplished in different countries, the following information (or similar information which it may be possible to supply under the laws and regulations of the country concerned):

(a) Records of convictions, together with any useful and available information with regard to the offender, such as his civil status, description, fingerprints, photography and police record, his methods of operations, etc.

(b) Particulars of any measures of refusal of admission or of expulsion which may have been applied to him.

These documents and information shall be sent direct and without delay to the authorities of the countries concerned in each particular case by the authorities named in Article I of the Agreement concluded in Paris on May 18th, 1904, and, if possible, in all cases when the offence, conviction, refusal of admission or expulsion has been duly established.

Article 4

If there should arise between the High Contracting Parties a dispute of any kind relating to the interpretation or application of the present Convention or of the Conventions of 1910 and 1921, and if such dispute cannot be satisfactorily settled by diplomacy, it shall be settled in accordance with any applicable agreements in force between the Parties providing for the settlement of international disputes.

In case there is no such agreement in force between the Parties, the dispute shall be referred to arbitration or judicial settlement. In the absence of agreement on the choice of another tribunal, the dispute shall, at the

request of any of the Parties, be referred to the
International Court of Justice, if all the Parties to the
dispute are Parties to the Statute of the International
Court of Justice, and if any of the Parties to the
dispute is not a Party to the Statute of the
International Court of Justice, to an arbitral tribunal
constituted in acccordance with the Hague Convention of
October 18th, 1907, for the Pacific Settlement of
International Disputes.

Article 5

The present Convention, of which the English and
French texts are both authoritative, shall bear this
day's date, and shall, until April 1st, 1934, be open for
signature on behalf of any Member of the League of
Nations, or of any non-member State which was represented
at the Conference which drew up this Convention or to
which the Council of the League of Nations shall have
communicated a copy of the Convention for this purpose.

Article 6

The present Convention shall be ratified. As from 1
January 1948 the instruments of ratification shall be
transmitted to the Secretary-General of the United
Nations, who shall notify their receipt to all Members of
the United Nations and to non-member States to which the
Secretary-General has communicated a copy of the
Convention.

Article 7

Members of the United Nations may accede to the
present Convention. The same applies to non-member
States to which the Economic and Social Council of the
United Nations may decide officially to communicate the
present Convention.

The instrument of accession shall be transmitted to
the Secretary-General of the United Nations, who shall
notify their receipt to all Members of the United Nations
and to non-member States to which the Secretary-General
has communicated a copy of the Convention.

Article 8

The present Convention shall come into force sixty days after the Secretary-General of the League of Nations has received two ratifications or accessions.

It shall be registered by the Secretary-General on the day of its entry into force.

Subsequent ratifications or accessions shall take effect at the end of sixty days after their receipt by the Secretary-General.

Article 9

The present Convention may be denounced by notification addressed to the Secretary-General of the United Nations. Such denunciation shall take effect one year after its receipt, but only in relation to the High Contracting Party who has notified it.

Article 10

The Secretary-General of the United Nations shall communicate to all the Members of the United Nations and to the non-member States to which the Secretary-General has communicated a copy of the Convention, the denunciations referred to in Article 9.

Table of Ratifications

Afghanistan+	4/19/35	Cuba+	6/25/36
Algeria+	10/31/63	Czechoslovakia+	7/27/35
Australia+	9/2/36	Finland+	12/21/36
Austria+	8/7/36	France	1/8/47
Belgium+	6/11/36	Germany,	
Benin	4/4/62	Democratic	
Brazil+	6/24/38	Republic of+*	7/16/74
Bulgaria	12/19/34	Greece+	8/20/37
Byelorussian		Hungary+	8/12/35
SSR	5/21/48	Iran	4/12/35
Central African		Ireland+	5/25/38
Republic	9/4/62	Ivory Coast+	12/8/61
Chile	3/20/35	Libyan Arab	
Congo	10/15/62	Jamahiriya+	2/17/59

Latvia	9/17/35	Singapore+	10/26/66
Luxembourg+	3/14/55	South Africa	
Madagascar+	2/12/64	(Union of	
Mali+	2/2/73	South Africa)+	11/20/35
Mexico+	5/3/38	Sudan	6/13/34
Netherlands+	9/20/35	Sweden+	6/25/34
Nicaragua+	12/12/35	Switzerland	7/17/34
Niger+	8/25/61	Turkey+	3/19/41
Norway+	6/26/35	Union of Soviet	
Philippines+	9/30/54	Socialist	
Poland+	12/8/37	Republics+	12/18/47
Portugal	1/7/37	United Republic	
Romania+	6/6/35	of Cameroon	10/27/61
Senegal	5/2/63		

*Indicates reservation and declaration at time of ratification

+Indicates State has accepted the 1947 Protocol Amending this Convention.

Source: United Nations, <u>Multilateral Treaties Deposited with the Secretary-General: Status as at 31 December 1981</u> (New York: United Nations, 1982).

8. Convention Concerning Equal Remuneration for Men and Women Workers for Work of Equal Value '

Background

The United Nations Commission on the Status of Women accepted "equal pay for equal work" as a major objective at its first session, in 1947. At the following session, the Commission adopted a resolution on this principle and asked the Economic and Social Council to invite the International Labour Organisation to begin serious study of the problem of promoting equal pay for equal work. The Universal Declaration of Human Rights in Article 23, paragraph 2, provided an early formulation of this right, and Article 7, paragraph a(i), of the International Covenant on Economic, Social and Cultural Rights codifies it.

Although the International Labour Organisation had included the principle in the preamble to its 1919 Constitution and that of 1948, as well, the General Conference decided to draft a special convention to codify it. The Equal Remuneration Convention was adopted by the General Conference on June 29, 1951, and it came into force on May 23, 1953, in accordance with Article 6, twelve months following its ratification by two members.

The treaty obligates States Parties to promote the principle of equal remuneration for work of equal value and to eliminate wage discrimination based on sex. It also requires national measures to promote objective appraisal of jobs, with the objective of eliminating job and wage discrimination.

Text

Preamble

The General Conference of the International Labour Organisation,

Having been convened at Geneva by the Governing Body of the International Labour Office, and having met in its Thirty-fourth Session on 6 June 1951, and

Having decided upon the adoption of certain proposals with regard to the principle of equal renumeration for men and women workers for work of equal value, which is the seventh item on the agenda of the session, and

Having determined that these proposals shall take the form of an international Convention,

adopts this twenty-ninth day of June of the year one thousand nine hundred and fifty-one the following Convention, which may be cited as the Equal Remuneration Convention, 1951:

Article 1

For the purpose of this Convention--

(a) the term "remuneration" includes the ordinary, basic or minimum wage or salary and any additional emoluments whatsoever payable directly or indirectly, whether in cash or in kind, by the employer to the worker and arising out of the workers' employment;

(b) the term "equal remuneration for men and women workers for work of equal value" refers to rates of remuneration established without discrimination based on sex.

Article 2

1. Each Member shall, by means appropriate to the methods in operation for determining rates of remuneration, promote and, in so far as is consistent with such methods, ensure the application to all workers of the principle of equal remuneration for men and women workers for work of equal value.

2. This principle may be applied by means of--

(a) national laws or regulations;

(b) legally established or recognised machinery for wage determination;

(c) collective agreements between employers and workers; or

(d) a combination of these various means.

Article 3

1. Where such action will assist in giving effect to the provisions of this Convention, measures shall be taken to promote objective appraisal of jobs on the basis of the work to be performed.

2. The methods to be followed in this appraisal may be decided upon by the authorities responsible for the determination of rates of remuneration, or, where such rates are determined by collective agreements, by the parties thereto.

3. Differential rates between workers, which correspond, without regard to sex, to differences, as determined by such objective appraisal, in the work to be performed, shall not be considered as being contrary to the principle of equal remuneration for men and women workers for work of equal value.

Article 4

Each Member shall co-operate as appropriate with the employers' and workers' organisations concerned for the purpose of giving effect to the provisions of this Convention.

Article 5

The formal ratifications of this Convention shall be communicated to the Director-General of the International Labour Office for registration.

Article 6

1. This Convention shall be binding only upon those
Members of the International Labour Organisation whose
ratifications have been registered with the
Director-General.

2. It shall come into force twelve months after the
date on which the ratifications of two Members have been
registered with the Director-General.

3. Thereafter, this Convention shall come into
force for any Member twelve months after the date on
which its ratification has been registered.

Article 7

1. Declarations communicated to the
Director-General of the International Labour Office in
accordance with paragraph 2 of Article 35 of the
Constitution of the International Labour Organization
shall indicate--

(a) the territories in respect of which the
    Member concerned undertakes that the
    provisions of the Convention shall be
    applied without modification;

(b) the territories in respect of which it
    undertakes that the provisions of the
    Convention shall be applied subject to
    modifications, together with details of the
    said modifications;

(c) the territories in respect of which the
    Convention is inapplicable and in such cases
    the grounds on which it is inapplicable;

(d) the territories in respect of which it
    reserves its decisions pending further
    consideration of the position.

2. The undertakings referred to in subparagraphs
(a) and (b) of paragraph 1 of this Article shall be
deemed to be an integral part of the ratification and
shall have the force of ratification.

3. Any Member may at any time by a subsequent declaration cancel in whole or in part any reservation made in its original declaration by virtue of subparagraphs (b), (c) or (d) of paragraph 1 of this Article.

4. Any Member may, at any time at which the Convention is subject to denunciation in accordance with the provisions of Article 9, communicate to the Director-General a declaration modifying in any other respect the terms of any former declaration and stating the present position in respect of such territories as it may specify.

Article 8

1. Declarations communicated to the Director-General of the International Labour Office in accordance with paragraphs 4 or 5 of Article 35 of the Constitution of the International Labour Organisation shall indicate whether the provisions of the Convention will be applied in the territory concerned without modification or subject to modification; when the declaration indicates that the provisions of the Convention will be applied subject to modifications, it shall give details of said modifications.

2. The Member, Members or international authority concerned may at any time by a subsequent declaration renounce in whole or in part the right to have recourse to any modification indicated in any former declaration.

3. The Member, Members or international authority concerned may, at any time at which this Convention is subject to denunciation in accordance with the provisions of Article 9, communicate to the Director-General a declaration modifying in any other respect the terms of any former declaration and stating the present position in respect of the application of the Convention.

Article 9

1. A Member which has ratified this Convention may denounce it after the expiration of ten years from the date on which the Convention first comes into force, by an act communicated to the Director-General of the

International Labour Office for registration. Such denunciation shall not take effect until one year after the date on which it is registered.

2. Each Member which has ratified this Convention and which does not, within the year following the expiration of the period of ten years mentioned in the preceding paragraph, exercise the right of denunciation provided for in this Article, will be bound for another period of ten years and, thereafter, may denounce this Convention at the expiration of each period of ten years under the terms provided for in this Article.

Article 10

1. The Director-General of the International Labour Office shall nofify all Members of the International Labour Organisation of the registration of all ratifications, declarations and denunciations communicated to him by the Members of the Organisation.

2. When notifying the Members of the Organisation of the registration of the second ratification communicated to him, the Director-General shall draw the attention of the Members of the Organisation to the date upon which the Convention will come into force.

Article 11

The Director-General of the International Labour Office shall communicate to the Secretary-General of the United Nations for registration in accordance with Article 102 of the Charter of the United Nations full particulars of all ratifications, declarations and acts of denunciation registered by him in accordance with the provisions of the preceding articles.

Article 12

At such times as it may consider necessary, the Governing Body of the International Labour Office shall present to the General Conference a report on the working of this Convention and shall examine the desirability of placing on the agenda of the Conference the question of its revision in whole or in part.

Article 13

1. Should the Conference adopt a new Convention revising this Convention in whole or in part, then, unless the new Convention otherwise provides--

(a) the ratification by a Member of the new revising Convention shall _ipso jure_ involve the immediate denunciation of this Convention, notwithstanding the provisions of Article 9 above, if and when the new revising Convention shall have come into force;

(b) as from the date when the new revising Convention comes into force this Convention shall cease to be open to ratification by the Members.

2. This Convention shall in any case remain in force in its actual form and content for those Members which have ratified it but have not ratified the revising Convention.

Article 14

The English and French versions of the text of this Convention are equally authoritative.

The foregoing is the authentic text of the Convention duly adopted by the General Conference of the International Labour Organisation during its Thirty-fourth Session which was held at Geneva and declared closed the twenty-ninth day of June 1951.

IN FAITH WHEREOF we have appended our signatures this second day of August 1951.

The President of the Conference:
Rappard

The Director-General of the International Labour Office:
David A. Morse

Table of Ratifications

Afghanistan	8/22/69	Indonesia	8/11/58
Albania	6/3/57	Iran	6/10/72
Algeria	10/19/62	Iraq	8/28/63
Angola	6/4/76	Ireland	12/18/74
Argentina	9/24/56	Israel	6/9/65
Australia	12/10/74	Italy	6/8/56
Austria	10/29/53	Ivory Coast	5/5/61
Barbados	9/19/74	Jamaica	1/14/75
Belgium	5/23/52	Japan	8/24/67
Benin	5/16/68	Jordan	9/22/66
Bolivia	11/15/73	Lebanon	6/1/77
Brazil	4/25/57	Libyan Arab	
Bulgaria	11/7/55	Jamahiriya	6/22/62
Byelorussian		Luxembourg	8/23/67
SSR	8/21/56	Madagascar	8/10/62
Canada	11/16/72	Malawi	3/22/65
Cape Verde	10/16/70	Mali	7/12/68
Central African		Mexico	8/23/52
Republic	6/9/64	Mongolia	6/3/69
Chad	3/29/66	Morocco	5/11/79
Chile	9/20/71	Mozambique	6/6/77
China	5/1/58	Nepal	6/10/76
Colombia	6/7/63	Netherlands	6/16/71
Comoros	10/23/78	Nicaragua	10/31/67
Costa Rica	6/2/60	Niger	8/9/66
Cuba	1/13/54	Nigeria	5/8/74
Czechoslovakia	10/30/57	Norway	9/24/59
Denmark	6/22/60	Panama	6/3/58
Djibouti	8/3/78	Paraguay	6/24/64
Dominican		Peru	2/1/60
Republic	9/22/53	Philippines	12/29/53
Ecuador	3/11/57	Poland	10/25/54
Egypt (U. A. R.)	7/26/60	Portugal	2/20/67
Finland	1/14/63	Romania	5/28/57
France	3/10/53	Rwanda	12/2/80
Gabon	6/13/61	Saudi Arabia	6/15/78
German Democratic		Senegal	10/22/62
Republic	5/7/75	Sierra Leone	11/15/68
Germany, Federal		Spain	11/6/67
Republic of	6/8/56	Sudan	10/22/70
Ghana	3/14/68	Swaziland	6/5/81
Greece	6/6/75	Sweden	6/20/62
Guatemala	8/2/61	Switzerland	10/25/72
Guinea	8/11/67	Syrian Arab	
Guinea-Bissau	2/21/77	Republic (Syria)	6/7/57
Guyana	6/13/75	Tunisia	10/11/68
Haiti	3/4/58	Turkey	7/19/67
Honduras	8/9/56	Ukrainian SSR	8/10/56
Hungary	6/8/56	Union of Soviet	
Iceland	2/17/58	Socialist	
India	9/25/58	Republics	4/30/56

United Kingdom of		Upper Volta	6/30/69
Great Britain and		Yemen	7/29/76
Northern Ireland	6/15/71	Yugoslavia	5/21/52
United Republic		Zaire	6/16/69
of Cameroon	5/25/70	Zambia	6/20/72

Source: International Labour Office, List of Ratifications of Conventions: As at 31 December 1981 (Geneva: International Labour Office, 1982).

9. Convention on the Political Rights of Women

Background

The General Assembly on December 11, 1946, adopted Resolution 56(I), recommending to Member States that they adopt legislation to provide women the same political rights as men; this action was taken to encourage fulfillment of their obligations under the Charter. The Universal Declaration of Human Rights of 1948 also provides in Article 21 that everyone, regardless of sex, has the right to participate in the government of his or her country and to have equal access to its public service.

This treaty was drafted by the United Nations Commission on the Status of Women. Inspired by the 1948 Convention on the Granting of Political Rights to Women, adopted by the Inter-American Conference, the Commission decided in 1949 to make political rights a top priority in their work. After completing the draft treaty, and submitting it to the Economic and Social Council, however, it was twice rejected on the grounds that the subject was inappropriate for international legal formulation and should instead be treated through social and educational programs. The Commission did succeed in getting the draft submitted to Member States for comment. Receipt of these responses occasioned no changes in the draft which was again submitted to the Economic and Social Council in May, 1952. This time it was accepted and sent to the General Assembly. The Convention was adopted by the General Assembly in Resolution 640 (VII) of December 20, 1952, by a vote of 46 to 0 with 11 abstentions. It came into force on July 7, 1954, in accordance with Article VI, on the ninetieth day following the deposit of the sixth instrument of ratification.

The treaty provides that women are entitled to vote, are eligible to stand for election, and may hold public office, all on equal terms with men. In pursuance of

Economic and Social Council resolution 540 E (XVI) of July 23, 1953, a voluntary reporting system was established whereby States Parties report biannually to the Council on measures they have taken to implement the treaty. In 1963 the reporting request was extended to include non-ratifying States and in 1972 the procedure was merged with the four year reporting system established by the Declaration on the Elimination of Discrimination Against Women.

Text

Preamble

The Contracting Parties,

Desiring to implement the principle of equality of rights for men and women contained in the Charter of the United Nations,

Recognizing that everyone has the right to take part in the government of his country, directly or indirectly through freely chosen representatives, and has the right to equal access to public service in his country, and desiring to equalize the status of men and women in the enjoyment and exercise of political rights, in accordance with the provisions of the Charter of the United Nations and of the Universal Declaration of Human Rights,

Having resolved to conclude a Convention for this purpose,

Hereby agree as hereinafter provided:

Article I

Women shall be entitled to vote in all elections on equal terms with men, without any discrimination.

Article II

Women shall be eligible for election to all publicly elected bodies, established by national law, on equal terms with men, without any discrimination.

Article III

Women shall be entitled to hold public office and to exercise all public functions, established by national law, on equal terms with men, without any discrimination.

Article IV

1. This Convention shall be open for signature on behalf of any Member of the United Nations and also on behalf of any other State to which an invitation has been addressed by the General Assembly.

2. This Convention shall be ratified and the instruments of ratification shall be deposited with the Secretary-General of the United Nations.

Article V

1. This Convention shall be open for accession to all States referred to in paragraph 1 of article IV.

2. Accession shall be effected by the deposit of an instrument of accession with the Secretary-General of the United Nations.

Article VI

1. This Convention shall come into force on the ninetieth day following the date of deposit of the sixth instrument of ratification or accession.

2. For each State ratifying or acceding to the Convention after the deposit of the sixth instrument of ratification or accession the Convention shall enter into force on the ninetieth day after deposit by such State of its instrument of ratification or accession.

Article VII

In the event that any State submits a reservation to any of the articles of this Convention at the time of signature, ratification or accession, the Secretary-General shall communicate the text of the reservation to all States which are or may become parties to this Convention. Any State which objects to the reservation may, within a period of ninety days from the date of the said communication (or upon the date of its becoming a party to the Convention), notify the Secretary-General that it does not accept it. In such case, the Convention shall not enter into force as between such State and the State making the reservation.

Article VIII

1. Any State may denounce this Convention by written notification to the Secretary-General of the United Nations. Denunciation shall take effect one year after the date of receipt of the notification by the Secretary-General.

2. This Convention shall cease to be in force as from the date when the denunciation which reduces the number of parties to less than six becomes effective.

Article IX

Any dispute which may arise between any two or more Contracting States concerning the interpretation or application of this Convention which is not settled by negotiation, shall at the request of any one of the parties to the dispute be referred to the International Court of Justice for decision, unless they agree to another mode of settlement.

Article X

The Secretary-General of the United Nations shall notify all Members of the United Nations and the non-member States contemplated in paragraph I of article IV of this Convention of the following:

(a) Signatures and instruments of ratifications received in accordance with article IV;

(b) Instruments of accession received in accordance with article V;

(c) The date upon which this Convention enters into force in accordance with article VI;

(d) Communications and notifications received in accordance with article VII;

(e) Notifications of denunciation received in accordance with paragraph 1 of article VIII;

(f) Abrogation in accordance with paragraph 2 of article VIII.

Article XI

1   This Convention, of which the Chinese, English, French, Russian and Spanish texts shall be equally authentic, shall be deposited in the archives of the United Nations.

2. The Secretary-General of the United Nations shall transmit a certified copy to all Members of the United Nations and to the non-member States contemplated in paragraph I of article IV.

IN FAITH WHEREOF the undersigned, being duly authorized thereto by their respective Governments, have signed the present Convention, opened for signature at New York, on the thirty-first day of March, one thousand nine hundred and fifty-three.

Table of Ratifications

Afghanistan	12/16/66	Jamaica	8/14/66
Albania*	5/12/55	Japan	7/13/55
Argentina*	2/27/61	Lao People's	
Australia*	12/10/74	Democratic	
Austria*	4/18/69	Republic	1/28/69
Bahamas	8/16/77	Lebanon	6/5/56
Barbados	1/12/73	Lesotho*	11/4/74
Belgium*	5/20/64	Liberia+	12/9/53
Bolivia	9/22/70	Luxembourg	11/1/76
Brazil	8/13/63	Madagascar	2/12/64
Bulgaria*	3/17/54	Malawi	6/29/66
Burma+	9/14/54	Mali	7/16/74
Byelorussian		Malta*	7/9/68
SSR*	8/11/54	Mauritania	5/4/76
Canada*	1/30/57	Mauritius*	7/18/69
Central African		Mexico*	3/23/81
Republic	9/4/62	Mongolia*	8/18/65
Chile	10/18/67	Morocco*	11/22/76
China	12/21/53	Nepal*	4/26/66
Congo	10/15/62	Netherlands*	7/30/71
Costa Rica	7/25/67	New Zealand*	5/22/68
Cuba	4/8/54	Nicaragua	1/17/57
Cyprus	11/12/68	Niger	12/7/64
Czechoslovakia*	4/6/55	Nigeria	11/17/80
Denmark*	7/7/54	Norway	8/24/56
Dominican		Pakistan	12/7/54
Republic	12/11/53	Paraguay+	12/16/53
Ecuador*	4/23/54	Peru	7/1/75
Egypt (U. A. R.)	9/8/81	Philippines	9/12/57
El Salvador+	6/24/53	Poland*	8/11/54
Ethiopia	1/21/69	Republic of Korea	6/23/59
Fiji*	6/12/72	Romania*	8/6/54
Finland*	10/6/58	Senegal	5/2/63
France	4/22/57	Sierra Leone*	7/25/62
Gabon	4/19/67	Solomon Islands	9/3/81
German Democratic		Spain*	1/14/74
Republic*	3/27/73	Swaziland*	7/20/70
Germany, Federal		Sweden	3/31/54
Republic of*	11/4/70	Thailand	11/30/54
Ghana	12/28/65	Trinidad and	
Greece	12/29/53	Tobago	6/24/66
Guatemala*	10/7/59	Tunisia*	1/24/68
Guinea	1/24/78	Turkey	1/26/60
Haiti	2/12/58	Ukrainian SSR*	11/15/54
Hungary*	1/20/55	Union of Soviet	
Iceland	6/30/54	Socialist	
India*	11/1/61	Republics*	5/3/54
Indonesia*	12/16/58	United Kingdom of	
Ireland*	11/14/68	Great Britain	
Israel	7/6/54	and N. Ireland*	2/24/67
Italy*	3/6/68		

United Republic		Uruguay+	5/26/53
of Tanzania	6/19/75	Yugoslavia	6/23/54
United States of		Zaire	10/12/77
America	4/8/76	Zambia	2/4/72

+Indicates signature only.

*Indicates one or more reservations or declarations made at the time of signature or ratification. Most of the reservations to this treaty were procedural rather than substantive. The objections were to the compulsory jurisdiction of the International Court of Justice (Article IX) and to the provision that formal objections to reservations would result in the treaty being inoperative as between the State making the reservation and the State making the objection (Article VII). The only substantive reservations in significant numbers were to Article III, entitling women to hold office and exercise public functions on equal terms with men; States reserved the right to discriminate on the basis of sex in armed forces, hereditary monarchy, and other areas.

Source: United Nations, Multilateral Treaties Deposited With The Secretary-General: Status as at 31 December 1981 (New York: United Nations, 1982).

10. Convention Concerning Maternity Protection

Background

The original Convention Concerning Maternity Protection was adopted by the International Labour Organisation in 1919. At its 35th Session in June, 1952, the General Conference considered a revised Convention text and a supplementary Recommendation prepared by the Office of the Director-General. The General Conference adopted the new Convention by a vote of 114 to 36 with 25 abstentions. The Recommendation was adopted by a vote of 112 to 31 with 29 abstentions. The treaty came into force on September 7, 1955, in accordance with Article 9, twelve months after the date on which the second ratification was registered with the Director-General.

The new treaty extends the coverage of its terms to include agricultural and nonindustrial undertakings as well as to women wage earners working at home. It also extends the period of maternity leave to twelve weeks, from six, and increases the flexibility with which it can be taken. The provisions on cash and medical benefits are clarified and the principle is added that the employer is not to be held individually liable for the costs of benefits. The new treaty also adds the requirement that employers allow mothers time for nursing at work which time is to be treated as part of the work day. The Recommendation has similar provisions but with higher and more precise standards.

Text

Preamble

The General Conference of the International Labour Organisation,

Having been convened at Geneva by the Governing Body
of the International Labour Office, and having met in its
Thirty-fifth Session on 4 June 1952, and

Having decided upon the adoption of certain
proposals with regard to maternity protection, which is
the seventh item on the agenda of the session, and

Having determined that these proposals shall take
the form of an international Convention,

adopts this twenty-eighth day of June of the year one
thousand nine hundred and fifty-two the following
Convention, which may be cited as the Maternity
Protection Convention (Revised), 1952.

Article 1

1. This Convention applies to women employed in
industrial undertakings and in nonindustrial and
agricultural occupations, including women wage earners
working at home.

2. For the purpose of this Convention, the term
"industrial undertaking" comprises public and private
undertakings and any branch thereof and includes
particularly--

(a) mines, quarries, and other works for the
extraction of minerals from the earth;

(b) undertakings in which articles are
manufactured, altered, cleaned, repaired,
ornamented, finished, adapted for sale,
broken up or demolished, or in which
materials are transformed, including
undertakings engaged in shipbuilding, or in
the generation, transformation or
transmission of electricity or motive power
of any kind;

(c) undertakings engaged in building and civil
engineering work, including constructional,
repair, maintenance, alteration and
demolition work;

(d) undertakings engaged in the transport of
passengers or goods by road, rail, sea,
inland waterway or air, including the

- 120 -

handling of goods at docks, quays, wharves, warehouses or airports.

3. For the purpose of this Convention, the term "non-industial occupations" includes all occupations which are carried on in or in connection with the following undertakings or services, whether public or private:

(a) commercial establishments;

(b) postal and telecommunication services;

(c) establishments and administrative services in which the persons employed are mainly engaged in clerical work;

(d) newspaper undertakings;

(e) hotels, boarding houses, restaurants, clubs, cafes and other refreshment houses;

(f) establishments for the treatment and care of the sick, infirm or destitute and of orphans;

(g) theatres and places of public entertainment;

(h) domestic work for wages in private households; and any other nonindustrial occupations to which the competent authority may decide to apply the provisions of the Convention.

4. For the purpose of this Convention, the term "agricultural occupations" includes all occupations carried on in agricultural undertakings, including plantations and large-scale industrialised agricultural undertakings.

5. In any case in which it is doubtful whether this Convention applies to an undertaking, branch of an undertaking or occupation, the question shall be determined by the competent authority after consultation with the representative organisations of employers and workers concerned where such exist.

6. National laws or regulations may exempt from the application of this Convention undertakings in which only members of the employer's family, as defined by national laws or regulations, are employed.

Article 2

For the purpose of this Convention, the term "woman" means any female person, irrespective of age, nationality, race or creed, whether married or unmarried, and the term "child" means any child whether born of marriage or not.

Article 3

1. A woman to whom this Convention applies shall, on the production of a medical certificate stating the presumed date of her confinement, be entitled to a period of maternity leave.

2. The period of maternity leave shall be at least twelve weeks, and shall include a period of compulsory leave after confinement.

3. The period of compulsory leave after confinement shall be prescribed by national laws or regulations, but shall in no case be less than six weeks; the remainder of the total period of maternity leave may be provided before the presumed date of confinement or following expiration of the compulsory leave period or partly before the presumed date of confinement and partly following the expiration of the compulsory leave period as may be prescribed by national laws or regulations.

4. The leave before the presumed date of confinement shall be extended by any period elapsing between the presumed date of confinement and the actual date of confinement and the period of compulsory leave to be taken after confinement shall not be reduced on that account.

5. In case of illness medically certified arising out of pregnancy, national laws or regulations shall provide for additional leave before confinement, the maximum duration of which may be fixed by the competent authority.

6. In case of illness medically certified arising out of confinement, the woman shall be entitled to an extension of the leave after confinement, the maximum duration of which may be fixed by the competent authority.

Article 4

1. While absent from work on maternity leave in accordance with the provisions of Article 3, the woman shall be entitled to receive cash and medical benefits.

2. The rates of cash benefit shall be fixed by national laws or regulations so as to ensure benefits sufficient for the full and healthy maintenance of herself and her child in accordance with a suitable standard of living.

3. Medical benefits shall include pre-natal, confinement and post-natal care by qualified midwives or medical practitioners as well as hospitalisation care where necessary; freedom of choice of doctor and freedom of choice between a public and private hospital shall be respected.

4. The cash and medical benefits shall be provided either by means of compulsory social insurance or by means of public funds; in either case they shall be provided as a matter of right to all women who comply with the prescribed conditions.

5. Women who fail to qualify for benefits provided as a matter of right shall be entitled, subject to the means test required for social assistance, to adequate benefits out of social assistance funds.

6. Where cash benefits provided under compulsory social insurance are based on previous earnings, they shall be at a rate of not less than two-thirds of the woman's previous earnings taken into account for the purpose of computing benefits.

7. Any contribution due under a compulsory social insurance scheme providing maternity benefits and any tax based upon payrolls which is raised for the purpose of providing such benefits shall, whether paid both by the employer and the employees or by the employer, be paid in respect of the total number of men and women employed by the undertakings concerned, without distinction of sex.

8. In no case shall the employer be individually liable for the cost of such benefits due to women employed by him.

Article 5

1. If a woman is nursing her child she shall be entitled to interrupt her work for this purpose at a time or times to be prescribed by national laws or regulations.

2. Interruptions of work for the purpose of nursing are to be counted as working hours and remunerated accordingly in cases in which the matter is governed by or in accordance with laws and regulations; in cases in which the matter is governed by collective agreement, the position shall be as determined by the relevant agreement.

Article 6

While a woman is absent from work on maternity leave in accordance with the provisions of Article 3 of this Convention, it shall not be lawful for her employer to give her notice of dismissal during such absence, or to give her notice of a dismissal at such a time that the notice would expire during such absence.

Article 7

1. Any Member of the International Labour Organisation which ratified this Convention may, by a declaration accompanying its ratification, provide for exceptions from the application of the the Convention in respect of--

(a) certain categories of nonindustrial occupations;

(b) occupations carried on in agricultural undertakings, other than plantations;

(c) domestic work for wages in private households;

(d) women wage earners working at home;

(e) undertakings engaged in the transport of passengers or goods by sea.

2. The categories of occupations or undertakings in respect of which the Member proposes to have recourse to the provisions of paragraph 1 of this Article shall be specified in the declaration accompanying its ratification.

3. Any Member which has made such a declaration may at any time cancel that declaration, in whole or in part, by a subsequent declaration.

4. Every Member for which a declaration made under paragraph 1 of this Article is in force shall indicate each year in its annual report upon the application of this Convention the position of its law and practice in respect of the occupations or undertakings to which paragraph 1 of this Article applies in virtue of the said declaration and the extent to which effect has been given or is proposed to be given to the Convention in respect of such occupations or undertakings.

5. At the expiration of five years from the first entry into force of this Convention, the Governing Body of the International Labour Office shall submit to the Conference a special report concerning the application of these exceptions, containing such proposals as it may think appropriate for further action in regard to the matter.

Article 8

The formal ratifications of this Convention shall be communicated to the Director-General of the International Labour Office for registration.

Article 9

1. This Convention shall be binding only upon those Members of the International Labour Organisation whose ratifications have been registered with the Director-General.

2. It shall come into force twelve months after the date on which the ratifications of two Members have been registered with the Director-General.

3. Thereafter, this Convention shall come into force for any Member twelve months after the date on which its ratification has been registered.

Article 10

1. Declarations communicated to the Director-General of the International Labour Office in accordance with paragraph 2 of Article 35 of the Constitution of the International Labour Organisation shall indicate--

(a) the territories in respect of which the Member concerned undertakes that the provisions of the Convention shall be applied without modification;

(b) the territories in respect of which it undertakes that the provisions of the Convention shall be applied subject to modifications, together with details of the said modifications;

(c) the territories in respect of which the Convention is inapplicable and in such cases the grounds on which it is inapplicable;

(d) the territories in respect of which it reserves its decision pending further considertation of the position.

2. The undertakings referred to in subparagraphs (a) and (b) of paragraph 1 of this Article shall be deemed to be an integral part of the ratification and shall have the force of ratification.

3. Any Member may at any time by a subsequent declaration cancel in whole or in part any reservation made in its original declaration in virtue of subparagraphs (b), (c) or (d) of paragraph 1 of this Article.

4. Any Member may, at any time at which the Convention is subject to denunciation in accordance with the provisions of Article 12, communicate to the Director-General a declaration modifying in any other respect the terms of any former declaration and stating the present position in respect of such territories as it may specify.

Article 11

1. Declarations communicated to the Director-General of the International Labour Office in accordance with paragraphs 4 and 5 of Article 35 of the Constitution of the International Labour Organisation shall indicate whether the provisions of the Convention will be applied in the territory concerned without modification or subject to modifications; when the declaration indicates that the provisions of the Convention will be applied subject to modifications, it shall give details of the said modifications.

2. The Member, Members or international authority concerned may at any time by a subsequent declaration renounce in whole or in part the right to have recourse to any modification indicated in any former declaration.

3. The Member, Members or international authority concerned may, at any time at which this Convention is subject to denunciation in accordance with the provisions of Article 12, communicate to the Director-Genral a declaration modifying in any other respect the terms of any former declaration and stating the present position in respect of the application of the Convention.

Article 12

1. A Member which has ratified this Convention may denounce it after the expiration of ten years from the date on which the Convention first comes into force, by an act communicated to the Director-General of the International Labour Office for registration. Such denunciation shall not take effect until one year after the date on which it is registered.

2. Each Member which has ratified this Convention and which does not within the year following the expiration of the period of then years mentioned in the preceding paragraph, exercise the right of denunciation provided for in this Article, will be bound for another period of ten years and, thereafter, may denounce this Convention at the expiration of each period of ten years under the terms provided for in this Article.

Article 13

1. The Director-General of the International Labour Office shall notify all Members of the International Labour Organisation of the registration of all ratifications, declarations and denunciations communicated to him by the Members of the Organisation.

2. When notifying the Members of the Organisation of the registration of the second ratification communicated to him, the Director-General shall draw the attention of the Members of the Organisation to the date upon which the Convention will come into force.

Article 14

The Director-General of the International Labour Office shall communicate to the Secretary-General of the United Nations for registration in accordance with Article 102 of the Charter of the United Nations full particulars of all ratifications, declarations and acts of denunciation registered by him in accordance with the provisions of the preceding Articles.

Article 15

At such times as it may consider necessary the Governing Body of the International Labour Office shall present to the General Conference a report on the working of this Convention and shall examine the desirability of placing on the agenda of the Conference the question of its revision in whole or in part.

Article 16

1. Should the Conference adopt a new Convention revising this Convention in whole or in part, then, unless the new Convention otherwise provides--

(a) the ratification by a Member of the new revising Convention shall _ipso_ _jure_ involve the immediate denunciation of this

Convention, notwithstanding the provisions
of Article 12 above, if and when the new
revising Convention shall have come into
force;

(b) as from the date when the new revising
Convention comes into force this Convention
shall cease to be open to ratification by
the Members.

2. This Convention shall in any case remain in
force in its actual form and content for those Members
which have ratified it but have not ratified the revising
Convention.

Article 17

The English and French versions of the text of this
Convention are equally authoritative.

The foregoing is the authentic text of the
Convention duly adopted by the General Conference of the
International Labour Organisation during its Thirty-fifth
Session which was held at Geneva and declared closed the
twenty-eighth day of June 1952.

IN FAITH WHEREOF we have appended our signatures
this fourth day of July 1952.

The President of the Conference:
Jose de Segadas Vianna

The Director-General of the International Labour Office:
David A. Morse

Tables of Ratifications

Maternity Protection Convention, 1919

Algeria	10/19/62	France	12/16/50
Argentina	11/30/33	Gabon	6/13/61
Bulgaria	2/14/22	Germany, Federal	
Central African		Republic of	10/31/27
Republic	9/6/64	Greece	11/19/20
Chile	9/15/25	Guinea	12/12/66
Colombia	6/20/33	Hungary	4/19/28
Cuba	8/6/28	Italy	10/22/52

Ivory Coast	5/5/61	Romania	2/13/21
Libyan Arab		Spain	7/4/23
Jamahiriya	5/27/71	United Republic	
Luxembourg	4/16/68	of Cameroon	5/25/70
Mauritania	11/8/63	Upper Volta	6/30/69
Nicaragua	4/12/34	Venezuela	11/20/44
Panama	6/3/58	Yugoslavia	4/1/27

Maternity Protection Convention (Revised), 1952

Austria*	12/4/69	Mongolia	6/3/69
Bolivia	11/15/73	Netherlands*	9/18/81
Brazil*	6/18/65	Poland	3/10/76
Byelorussian		Netherlands	9/18/81
SSR	11/6/56	Poland	3/10/76
Cuba	9/7/54	Spain*	8/17/83
Ecuador	2/5/62	Ukrainian SSR	9/14/56
German Democratic		Union of Soviet	
Republic	6/19/79	Socialist	
Hungary	6/8/56	Republics	8/10/56
Italy	5/5/71	Uruguay	3/18/54
Libyan Arab		Yugoslavia	4/30/55
Jamahiriya	6/19/75	Zambia	10/23/79
Luxembourg	12/10/69		

*Indicates one or more reservations to the Convention.

Source: International Labour Conference, List of Ratifications of Convention: As at 31 December 1981 (Geneva: International Labour Office, 1982).

11. Supplementary Convention on the Abolition of Slavery, the Slave Trade, and Institutions and Practices Similar to Slavery

Background

The Economic and Social Council in 1955 appointed a committee to prepare a draft supplementing the 1926 Slavery Convention. The Committee met and completed a draft proposal in 1956. The Council then called a conference of plenipotentiaries which approved the convention on September 7, 1956. The treaty came into force on April 30, 1957, in accordance with Article 13, on the date of the second ratification.

The Convention obligates States Parties to take steps to abolish, as soon as possible, a set of institutions and practices which include: debt bondage; serfdom; child betrothal; and marital practices in which a woman is treated as property by her own or her husband's family or is liable to be inherited at her husband's death.

Text

Preamble

The States Parties to the present Convention,

Considering that freedom is the birthright of every human being,

Mindful that the peoples of the United Nations reaffirmed in the Charter their faith in the dignity and worth of the human person,

Considering that the Universal Declaration of Human Rights, proclaimed by the General Assembly of the United Nations as a common standard of achievement for all peoples and all nations, states that no one shall be held in slavery or servitude and that slavery and the slave trade shall be prohibited in all their forms,

Recognizing that, since the conclusion of the Slavery Convention signed at Geneva on 25 September 1926, which was designed to secure the abolition of slavery and of the slave trade, further progress has been made towards this end,

Having regard to the Forced Labour Convention of 1930 and to subsequent action by the International Labour Organisation in regard to forced or compulsory labour,

Being aware, however, that slavery, the slave trade and institutions and practices similar to slavery have not yet been eliminated in all parts of the world,

Having decided, therefore, that the Convention of 1926, which remains operative, should now be augmented by the conclusion of a supplementary convention designed to intensify national as well as international efforts towards the abolition of slavery, the slave trade and institutions and practices similar to slavery,

Having agreed as follows:

SECTION I

INSTITUTIONS AND PRACTICES

SIMILAR TO SLAVERY

Article 1

Each of the States Parties to this Convention shall take all practicable and necessary legislative and other measures to bring about progressively and as soon as possible the complete abolition or abandonment of the following institutions and practices, where they still exist and whether or not they are covered by the definition of slavery contained in article 1 of the Slavery Convention signed at Geneva on 25 September 1926:

    (a) Debt bondage, that is to say, the status or condition arising from a pledge by a debtor of his personal services or of those of a person under his control as security for a debt, if the value of those services as reasonably assessed is not applied towards the liquidation of the debt or the length and nature of those services are not respectively limited and defined;

(b) Serfdom, that is to say, the condition or status of a tenant who is by law, custom or agreement bound to live and labour on land belonging to another person and to render to such other person, some determinate service, whether for reward or not, and is not free to change his status;

(c) Any institution or practice whereby:

   (i) A woman, without the right to refuse, is promised or given in marriage on payment of a consideration in money or in kind to her parents, guardian, family or any other person or group; or

   (ii) The husband of a woman, his family, or his clan, has the right to transfer her to another person for value received or otherwise; or

   (iii) A woman on the death of her husband is liable to be inherited by another person;

(d) Any institution or practice whereby a child or young person under the age of 18 years, is delivered by either or both of his natural parents or by his guardian to another person, whether for reward or not, with a view to the exploitation of the child or young person or of his labour.

Article 2

With a view to bringing to an end the institutions and practices mentioned in article 1 (c) of this Convention, the States Parties undertake to prescribe, where appropriate, suitable minimum ages of marriage, to encourage the use of facilities whereby the consent of both parties to a marriage may be freely expressed in the presence of a competent civil or religious authority, and to encourage the registration of marriages.

SECTION II

THE SLAVE TRADE

Article 3

1. The act of conveying or attempting to convey slaves from one country to another by whatever means of transport, or of being accessory thereto, shall be a criminal offence under the laws of the States Parties to this Convention and persons convicted thereof shall be liable to very severe penalties.

2. (a) The States Parties shall take all effective measures to prevent ships and aircraft authorised to fly their flags from conveying slaves and to punish persons guilty of such acts or of using national flags for that purpose.

(b) The State Parties shall take all effective measures to ensure that their ports, airfields and coasts are not used for the conveyance of slaves.

3. The States Parties to this Convention shall exchange information in order to ensure the practical co-ordination of the measures taken by them in combating the slave trade and shall inform each other of every case of the slave trade, and of every attempt to commit this criminal offence, which comes to their notice.

Article 4

Any slave who takes refuge on board any vessel of a State Party to the Convention shall *ipso* *facto* be free.

SECTION III

SLAVERY AND INSTITUTIONS AND PRACTICES

SIMILAR TO SLAVERY

Article 5

In a country where the abolition or abandonment of slavery, or of the institutions or practices mentioned in article 1 of this Convention, is not yet complete, the act of mutilating, branding or otherwise marking a slave or a person of servile status in order to indicate his status, or as a punishment, or for any other reason, or of being accessory thereto, shall be a crimial offence under the laws of the States Parties to this Convention and persons convicted thereof shall be liable to punishment.

Article 6

1. The act of enslaving another person or of inducing another person to give himself or a person dependent upon him into slavery, or of attempting these acts, or being accessory thereto, or being a party to a conspiracy to accomplish any such acts, shall be a criminal offence under the laws of the States Parties to this Convention and persons convicted thereof shall be liable to punishment.

2. Subject to the provisions of the introductory paragraph of article 1 of this Convention, the provisions of paragraph 1 of the present article shall also apply to the act of inducing another person to place himself or a person dependent upon him into the servile status resulting from any of the institutions or practices mentioned in article 1, to any attempt to perform such acts, to bring accessory thereto, and to being a party to a conspiracy to accomplish any such acts.

SECTION IV

DEFINITIONS

Article 7

For the purposes of the present Convention:

(a) "Slavery" means, as defined in the Slavery
Convention of 1926, the status or condition
of a person over whom any or all of the
powers attaching to the right of ownership
are exercised, and "slave" means a person in
such condition or status;

(b) "A person of servile status" means a person
in the condition or status resulting from
any of the institutions or practices
mentioned in article 1 of this Convention;

(c) "Slave trade" means and includes all acts
involved in the capture, acquisition or
disposal of a person with intent to reduce
him to slavery; all acts involved in the
acquisition of a slave with a view to
selling or exchanging him; all acts of
disposal by sale or exchange of a person
acquired with a view to being sold or
exchanged; and, in general, every act of
trade or transport in slaves by whatever
means of conveyance.

SECTION V

CO-OPERATION BETWEEN STATES PARTIES AND

COMMUNICATION OF INFORMATION

Article 8

1. The States Parties to this Convention undertake
to co-operate with each other and with the United Nations
to give effect to the foregoing provisions.

2. The Parties undertake to communicate to the Secretary-General of the United Nations copies of any laws, regulations and administrative measures enacted or put into effect to implement the provisions of this Convention.

3. The Secretary-General shall communicate the information received under paragraph 2 of this article to the other Parties and to the Economic and Social Council as part of the documentation for any discussion which the Council might undertake with a view to making further recommendations for the abolition of slavery, the slave trade or the institutions and practices which are the subject of this Convention.

SECTION VI

FINAL CLAUSES

Article 9

No reservations may be made to this Convention.

Article 10

Any dispute between States Parties to this Convention relating to its interpretation or application, which is not settled by negotiation, shall be referred to the International Court of Justice at the request of any one of the parties to the dispute, unless the parties concerned agree on another mode of settlement.

Article 11

1. This Convention shall be open until 1 July 1957 for signature by any State Member of the United Nations or of a specialized agency. It shall be subject to ratification by the signatory States, and the instruments of ratification shall be deposited with the Secretary-General of the United Nations, who shall inform each signatory and acceding State.

2. After 1 July 1957 this Convention shall be open for accession by any State Member of the United Nations or of a specialized agency, or by any other State to which an invitation to accede has been addressed by the General Assembly of the United Nations. Accession shall be effected by the deposit of a formal instrument with the Secretary-General of the United Nations, who shall inform each signatory and acceding State.

Article 12

1. This Convention shall apply to all non-self-governing trust, colonial and other non-metropolitan territories for the international relations of which any State Party is responsible; the Party concerned shall, subject to the provisions of paragraph 2 of this article, at the time of signature, ratification or accession declare the non-metropolitan territory or territories to which the Convention shall apply ipso facto as a result of such signature, ratification or accession.

2. In any case in which the previous consent of a non-metropolitan territory is required by the constitutional laws or practices of the Party or of the non-metropolitan territory, the Party concerned shall endeavour to secure the needed consent of the non-metropolitan territory within the period of twelve months from the date of signature of the Convention by the metropolitan State, and when such consent has been obtained the Party shall notify the Secretary-General. This Convention shall apply to the territory or territories named in such notification from the date of its receipt by the Secretary-General.

3. After the expiry of the twelve-month period mentioned in the preceding paragraph, the States Parties concerned shall inform the Secretary-General of the results of the consultations with those non-metropolitan territories for whose international relations they are responsible and whose consent to the application of this Convention may have been withheld.

Article 13

1. This Convention shall enter into force on the date on which two States have become Parties thereto.

2. It shall thereafter enter into force with respect to each State and territory on the date of deposit of the instrument of ratification or accession of that State or notification of application to that territory.

Article 14

1. The application of this Convention shall be divided into successive periods of three years, of which the first shall begin on the date of entry into force of the Convention in accordance with paragraph 1 of article 13.

2. Any State Party may denounce this Convention by a notice addressed by that State to the Secretary-General not less than six months before the expiration of the current three-year period. The Secretary-General shall notify all other Parties of each such notice and the date of the receipt thereof.

3. Denunciations shall take effect at the expiration of the current three-year period.

4. In cases where, in accordance with the provisions of article 12, this Convention has become applicable to a non-metropolitan territory of a Party, that Party may at any time thereafter, with the consent of the territory concerned, give notice to the Secretary-General of the United Nations denouncing this Convention separately in respect of that territory. The denunciation shall take effect one year after the date of the receipt of such notice by the Secretary-General, who shall notify all other Parties of such notice and the date of the receipt thereof.

Article 15

This Convention, of which the Chinese, English, French, Russian and Spanish texts are equally authentic, shall be deposited in the archives of the United Nations Secretariat. The Secretary-General shall prepare a certified copy thereof for communication to States Parties to this Convention, as well as to all other States Members of the United Nations and of the specialized agencies.

IN WITNESS WHEREOF the undersigned, being duly authorized thereto by their respective Governments, have signed this Convention on the date appearing opposite their respective signatures.

DONE at the European Office of the United Nations at Geneva, this seventh day of September one thousand nine hundred and fifty-six.

Table of Ratifications

Afghanistan	11/16/66	El Salvador+	9/7/56
Albania	11/6/58	Ethiopia	1/21/69
Algeria	10/31/63	Fiji	6/12/72
Argentina	8/13/64	Finland	4/1/59
Australia	1/6/58	France	5/26/64
Austria	10/7/63	German Democratic	
Bahamas	6/10/76	Republic	7/16/74
Barbados	8/9/72	Germany, Federal	
Belgium	12/13/62	Republic of	1/14/59
Brazil	1/6/66	Ghana	5/3/63
Bulgaria	8/21/58	Greece	12/13/72
Byelorussian		Guatemala+	9/7/56
SSR	6/5/67	Guinea	3/14/77
Canada	1/10/63	Haiti	2/12/58
Central African		Hungary	2/26/58
Republic	12/30/70	Iceland	11/17/65
China	5/28/59	India	6/23/60
Congo	8/25/77	Iran	12/30/59
Cuba	8/21/63	Iraq	9/30/63
Cyprus	5/11/62	Ireland	9/18/61
Czechoslovakia	6/13/58	Israel+	10/23/57
Democratic		Italy	2/12/58
Kampuchea	6/12/57	Ivory Coast	12/10/70
Denmark	4/24/58	Jamaica	7/30/64
Djibouti	3/21/79	Jordan	9/27/57
Dominican		Kuwait	1/18/63
Republic	10/31/62	Lao People's	
Ecuador	3/29/60	Democratic	
Egypt (U. A. R.)	4/17/58	Republic	9/9/57

Lesotho	11/4/74	Singapore	3/28/72
Liberia+	9/7/56	Solomon Islands	11/3/81
Luxembourg	5/1/67	Spain	11/21/67
Madagascar	2/29/72	Sri Lanka	3/21/58
Malawi	8/2/65	Sudan	9/9/57
Malaysia	11/18/57	Suriname	10/12/79
Mali	2/2/73	Sweden	10/28/59
Malta	1/3/66	Switzerland	7/28/64
Mauritius	7/18/69	Syrian Arab	
Mexico	6/30/59	Republic (Syria)	4/17/58
Mongolia	12/20/68	Togo	7/8/80
Morocco	5/11/59	Trinidad and	
Nepal	1/7/63	Tobago	4/11/66
Netherlands	12/3/57	Tunisia	7/15/66
New Zealand	4/26/62	Turkey	7/17/64
Niger	7/22/63	Uganda	8/12/64
Nigeria	6/26/61	Ukrainian SSR	12/3/58
Norway	5/3/60	Union of Soviet	
Pakistan	3/20/58	Socialist	
Peru+	9/7/56	Republics	4/12/57
Philippines	11/17/64	United Kingdom of	
Poland	1/10/63	Great Britain and	
Portugal	8/10/59	Northern Ireland	4/30/57
Romania	11/13/57	United Republic	
Saint Vincent and		of Tanzania	11/28/62
the Grenadines	11/9/81	United States of	
San Marino+	9/16/75	America	12/6/67
Saudi Arabia	7/5/73	Yugoslavia	5/20/58
Senegal	7/19/79	Zaire	2/28/75
Sierra Leone	3/13/62	Zambia	3/26/73

+Indicates signature only.

Source: United Nations, Multilateral Treaties Deposited with the Secretary-General Status as at 31 December 1981 (New York: United Nations, 1982).

12. Convention on the Nationality of Married Women

Background

The nationality problems faced by married women were addressed in part by the 1930 Hague Convention on the Conflict of Nationality Laws and the 1933 Montevideo Convention on the Nationality of Women. The Commission on the Status of Women in January, 1948, asked the Economic and Social Council to request the Secretary-General to prepare a report on existing treaties on nationality and on the governmental replies to a questionnaire on the legal status and treatment of women. The Commission recognized the difficulties faced by many women married to men of nationalities different from their own. Often national laws deprived them of personal rights and deprived them of their own nationality. In some States the husband's nationality was automatically conferred at marriage, at times automatically lost at divorce. Other States' laws could leave a women stateless, by depriving her of her own nationality at marriage, but prohibiting her , by law , from acquiring the nationality of her husband.

At their 1949 session, the Commission, responding to the serious problems reflected in the Secretary-General's report, decided that a convention on the nationality of married women should be a priority. By 1955 a treaty had been drafted and sent to the Economic and Social Council which approved and then forwarded it to the General Assembly. The treaty was adopted by the General Assembly in Resolution 1040 (XI) on January 29, 1957, by a vote of 47 to 2 with 24 abstentions. It entered into force on August 11, 1958, in accordance with Article 6, ninety days following the deposit of the sixth instrument of ratification.

In 1954 the Secretary-General began a regular system of collecting information on changes in the legislation affecting the nationality of married women; this system was later merged with that which the Commission on the

Status of Women had established in connection with the Declaration on the Elimination of Discrimination Against Women.

Continuing a principle established in the Hague Convention, this treaty emphasizes the independence of the nationality of the wife from that of her husband, rather than the traditional principle of family unity. The States Parties accept, with respect to their nationals, that celebration or dissolution of a marriage or a change of nationality by the husband, will not automatically affect the nationality of the wife. They also agree to establish special naturalization procedures to allow a wife to acquire the nationality of her husband if she so desires.

Text

Preamble

The Contracting States,

Recognizing that conflicts in law and in practice with reference to nationality arise as a result of provisions concerning the loss or acquisition of nationality by women as a result of marriage, of its dissolution, or of the change of nationality by the husband during marriage,

Recognizing that, in article 15 of the Universal Declaration of Human Rights, the General Assembly of the United Nations has proclaimed that "everyone has the right to a nationality" and that "no one shall be arbitrarily deprived of his nationality nor denied the right to change his nationality",

Desiring to co-operate with the United Nations in promoting universal respect for, and observance of, human rights and fundamental freedoms for all without distinction as to sex,

Hereby agree as hereinafter provided:

Article 1

Each Contracting State agrees that neither the celebration nor the dissolution of a marriage between one of its nationals and an alien, nor the change of nationality by the husband during marriage, shall automatically affect the nationality of the wife.

Article 2

Each Contracting State agrees that neither the voluntary acquisition of the nationality of another State nor the renunciation of its nationality by one of its nationals shall prevent the retention of its nationality by the wife of such national.

Article 3

1. Each Contracting State agrees that the alien wife of one of its nationals may, at her request, acquire the nationality of her husband through specially privileged naturalization procedures; the grant of such nationality may be subject to such limitations as may be imposed in the interests of national security or public policy.

2. Each Contracting State agrees that the present Convention shall not be construed as affecting any legislation or judicial practice by which the alien wife of one of its nationals may, at her request, acquire her husband's nationality as a matter of right.

Article 4

1. The present Convention shall be open for signature and ratification on behalf of any State Member of the United Naions and also on behalf of any other State which is or hereafter becomes a member of any specialized agency of the United Nations, or which is or hereafter becomes a Party to the Statute of the International Court of Justice, or any other State to which an invitation has been addressed by the General Assembly of the United Nations.

- 144 -

2. The present Convention shall be ratified and the instruments of ratification shall be deposited with the Secretary-General of the United Nations.

Article 5

1. The present Convention shall be open for accession to all States referred to in paragraph 1 of article 4.

2. Accession shall be effected by the deposit of an instrument of accession with the Secretary-General of the United Nations.

Article 6

1. The present Convention shall come into force on the ninetieth day following the date of deposit of the sixth instrument of ratification or accession.

2. For each State ratifying or acceding to the Convention after the deposit of the sixth instrument of ratification or accession, the Convention shall enter into force on the ninetieth day after deposit by such State of its instrument of ratification or accession.

Article 7

1. The present Convention shall apply to all non-self-governing, trust, colonial and other non-metropolitan territories for the international relations of which any Contracting State is responsible; the Contracting State concerned shall, subject to the provisions of paragraph 2 of the present article, at the time of signature, ratification or accession, declare the non-metropolitan territory or territories to which the Convention shall apply ipso facto as a result of such signature, ratification or accession.

2. In any case in which, for the purpose of nationality, a non-metropolitan territory is not treated as one with the metropolitan territory, or in any case in which the previous consent of a non-metropolitan

territory is required by the constitutional laws or practices of the Contracting State or of the non-metropolitan territory for the application of the Convention to that territory, that Contracting State shall endeavour to secure the needed consent of the non-metropolitan territory within the period of twelve months from the date of signature of the Convention by that Contracting State, and when such consent has been obtained the Contracting State shall notify the Secretary-General of the United Nations. The present Convention shall apply to the territory or territories named in such notification from the date of its receipt by the Secretary-General.

3. After the expiry of the twelve-month period mentioned in paragraph 2 of the present article, the Contracting States concerned shall inform the Secretary-General of the results of the consultations with those non-metropolitan territories for whose international relations they are responsible and whose consent to the application of the present Convention may have been withheld.

Article 8

1. At the time of signature, ratification or accession, any State may make reservations to any article of the present Convention other than articles 1 and 2.

2. If any State makes a reservation in accordance with paragraph 1 of the present article, the Convention, with the exception of those provisions to which the reservation relates, shall have effect as between the reserving State and the other Parties. The Secretary-General of the United Nations shall communicate the text of the reservation to all States which are or may become Parties to the Convention. Any State Party to the convention or which thereafter becomes a Party may notify the Secretary-General that it does not agree to consider itself bound by the Convention with respect to the State making the reservation. This notification must be made, in the case of a State already a Party, within ninety days from the date of the communication by the Secretary-General; and, in the case of a State subsequently becoming a Party, within ninety days from the date when the instrument of ratification or accession is deposited. In the event that such a notification is made, the Convention shall not be deemed to be in effect as between the State making the notification and the State making the reservation.

3. Any State making a reservation in accordance with paragraph 1 of the present article may at any time withdraw the reservation, in whole or in part, after it has been accepted, by a notification to this effect addressed to the Secreatary-General of the United Nations. Such notification shall take effect on the date on which it is received.

Article 9

1. Any Contracting State may denounce the present Convention by written notification to the Secretary-General of the United Nations. Denunciation shall take effect one year after the date or receipt of the notification by the Secretary-General.

2. The present Convention shall cease to be in force as from the date when the denunciation which reduces the number of Parties to less than six becomes effective.

Article 10

Any dispute which may arise between any two or more Contracting States concerning the interpretation or application of the present Convention, which is not settled by negotiation, shall, at the request of any one of the Parties to the dispute, be referred to the International Court of Justice for decision, unless the Parties agree to another mode of settlement.

Article 11

The Secretary-General of the United Nations shall notify all States Members of the United Nations and the non-member States contemplated in paragraph 1 of article 4 of the present Convention of the following:

(a) Signatures and instruments of ratification received in accordance with article 4;

(b) Instruments of accession received in accordance with article 5;

(c) The date upon which the present Convention enters into force in accordance with article 6;

(d) Communications and notifications received in accordance with article 8;

(e) Notifications of denunciation received in accordance with paragraph 1 of article 9;

(f) Abrogation in accordance with paragraph 2 of article 9.

Article 12

1   The present Convention, of which the Chinese, English,   French,   Russian and Spanish texts shall be equally authentic,   shall be deposited in the archives of the United Nations.

2. The Secretary-General of the United Nations shall transmit a certified copy of the Convention to all States Members of the United Nations and to the non-member States contemplated in paragraph 1 or article 4.

IN FAITH WHEREOF the undersigned, being duly authorized thereto by their respective Governments, have signed the present Convention, opened for signature at New York, on the 20th day of February, one thousand nine hundred and fifty-seven.

Table of Ratifications

Albania	7/27/60	Colombia+	2/20/57
Argentina*	10/10/63	Cuba	12/5/57
Australia	3/14/61	Cyprus	4/26/71
Austria	1/19/68	Czechoslovakia	4/5/62
Bahamas	6/10/76	Denmark	6/22/59
Barbados	10/26/79	Dominican	
Belgium+	5/15/72	Republic	10/10/57
Brazil*	12/4/68	Ecuador	3/29/60
Bulgaria	6/22/60	Fiji	6/12/72
Byelorussian		Finland	5/15/68
SSR	12/23/58	German Democratic	
Canada	10/21/59	Republic*	12/27/73
Chile+*	3/18/57	Germany, Federal	
China	9/22/58	Republic of	2/7/74

Ghana	8/15/66	Romania	12/2/60
Guatemala*	7/13/60	Sierra Leone	3/13/62
Guinea+	3/19/75	Singapore	3/18/66
Hungary	12/3/59	Sri Lanka	5/30/58
Iceland	10/18/77	Swaziland	9/18/70
India+*	5/15/57	Sweden	5/13/58
Ireland	11/25/57	Trinidad and	
Israel	6/7/57	Tobago	4/11/66
Jamaica	7/30/64	Tunisia*	1/24/68
Lesotho	11/4/74	Uganda	4/15/65
Luxembourg	7/22/77	Ukrainian SSR	12/3/58
Malawi	9/8/66	Union of Soviet	
Malaysia	2/24/59	Socialist	
Mali	2/2/73	Republics	9/17/58
Malta	6/7/67	United Kingdom of	
Mauritius	7/18/69	Great Britain and	
Mexico	4/4/79	Northern Ireland	8/28/57
Netherlands	8/8/66	United Republic	
New Zealand	12/17/58	of Tanzania	11/28/62
Norway	5/20/58	Uruguay+*	2/20/57
Pakistan+	4/10/58	Yugoslavia	3/13/59
Poland	7/3/59	Zambia	1/22/75
Portugal+	2/21/57		

+Indicates signature only.

*Indicates reservation or declaration at time of signature or ratification.

Source: United Nations, Multilateral Treaties Deposited with the Secretary-General: Status as at 31 December 1981 (New York: United Nations, 1982).

13. Convention Concerning Condition of Employment of Plantation Workers

Background

The International Labour Organisation established a special tripartite committee to consider Work on Plantations and in 1957 established a Conference Committee to draft international regulations addressing the conditions of Plantation Workers. The members representing employers felt the needs of Plantation Workers were met under general regulations already established; the workers' representatives, however, wanted special regulations on the subject. They felt that a separate treaty would expedite the application of the already existing regulations to those involved in plantation work. This latter approach was adopted; both a Convention and a Recommendation were suggested as suitable forms. The Convention was adopted on June 24, 1958. It came into force on January 22, 1960, in accordance with Article 93, six months after the registration of two instruments of ratification. The Convention addresses a wide range of subjects drawing together regulations from a variety of other International Labour Organisation agreements and focusing them specifically on Plantation Workers. The Maternity Protection section follows the lines of the earlier Maternity Protection Convention. States may ratify selected operative parts of the Convention.

Text (Excerpts)

Preamble

The General Conference of the International Labour Organisation,

Having been convened at Geneva by the Governing Body of the International Labour Office, and having met in its Forty-second Session on 4 June 1958, and

Having considered the question of conditions of employment of plantation workers, which is the fifth item on the agenda of the session, and

Having decided that, as an exceptional measure, in order to expedite the application to plantations of certain provisions of existing Conventions, pending the more general ratification of these Conventions and the application and the application of their provisions to all persons within their scope, and to provide for the application to plantations of certain Conventions not at present applicable thereto, it is desirable to adopt an instrument for these purposes, and

Having determined that this instrument shall take the form of an international Convention,

adopts this twenty-fourth day of June of the year one thousand nine hundred and fifty-eight the following Convention, which may be cited as the Plantations Convention, 1958:

PART I.   GENERAL PROVISIONS

Article 1

1. For the purpose of this Convention, the term "plantation" includes any agricultural undertaking regularly employing hired workers which is situated in the tropical or subtropical regions and which is mainly concerned with the cultivation or production for commercial purposes of coffee, tea, sugarcane, rubber, bananas, cocoa, coconuts, groundnuts, cotton, tobacco, fibres (sisal, jute and hemp), citrus, palm oil, cinchona or pineapple; it does not include family or small-scale holdings producing for local consumption and not regularly employing hired workers.

2. Each Member for which this Convention is in force may, after consultation with the most representative organisations of employers and workers concerned, where such exist, make the Convention applicable to other plantations by--

(a) adding to the list of crops referred to in paragraph 1 of this Article any one or more of the following crops: rice, chicory, cardamom, geranium and pyrethrum, or any other crop;

(b) adding to the plantations covered by paragraph 1 of this Article classes of undertakings not referred to therein which, by national law or practice, are classified as plantations;

and shall indicate the action taken in its annual reports upon the application of the Convention submitted under article 22 of the Constitution of the International Labour Organisation.

3. For the purpose of this Article the term "plantation" shall ordinarily include services carrying out the primary processing of the product or products of the plantation.

Article 2

Each Member which ratifies this Convention undertakes to apply its provisions equally to all plantation workers without distinction as to race, colour, sex, religion, political opinion, nationality, social origin, tribe or trade union membership.

* * * * *

PART VII   MATERNITY PROTECTION

Article 46

For the purpose of this Part of this Convention, the term "woman" means any female person, irrespective of age, nationality, race or creed, whether married or unmarried, and the term "child" means any child whether born of marriage or not.

Article 47

1. A woman to whom this Part of this Convention applies shall, on the production of appropriate evidence of the presumed date of her confinement, be entitled to a period of maternity leave.

2. The competent authority may, after consultation with the most representative organisations of employers and workers, where such exist, prescribe a qualifying period for maternity leave which shall not exceed a total of 150 days of employment with the same employer during the 12 months preceding the confinement.

3. The period of maternity leave shall be at least 12 weeks, and shall include a period of compulsory leave after confinement.

4. The period of compulsory leave after confinement shall be prescribed by national laws or regulations, but shall in no case be less than six weeks; the remainder of the total period of maternity leave may be provided before the presumed date of confinement or following expiration of the compulsory leave period or partly before the presumed date of confinement and partly following the expiration of the compulsory leave period as may be prescribed by national laws or regulations.

5. The leave before the presumed date of confinement shall be extended by any period elapsing between the presumed date of confinement and the actual date of confinement, and the period of compulsory leave to be taken after confinement shall not be reduced on that account.

6. In case of illness suitably certified as arising out of pregnancy national laws or regulations shall provide for additional leave before confinement, the maximum duration of which may be fixed by the competent authority.

7. In case of illness suitably certified as arising out of confinement the women shall be entitled to an extension of the leave after confinement, the maximum duration of which may be fixed by the competent authority.

8. No pregnant woman shall be required to undertake any type of work harmful to her in the period prior to her maternity leave.

Article 48

1. While absent from work on maternity leave in accordance with the provisions of Article 47, the woman shall be entitled to receive cash and medical benefits.

2. The rates of cash benefit shall be fixed by national laws or regulations so as to ensure benefits sufficient for the full and healthy maintenance of herself and her child in accordance with a suitable standard of living.

3. Medical benefits shall include prenatal, confinement and postnatal care by qualified midwives or medical practitioners as well as hospitalisation care where necessary; freedom of choice of doctor and freedom of choice between a public and private hospital shall be respected as far as practicable.

4. Any contribution due under a compulsory social insurance scheme providing maternity benefits and any tax based upon payrolls which is raised for the purpose of providing such benefits shall, whether paid both by the employer and the employees or by the employer, be paid in respect of the total number of men and women employed by the undertakings concerned, without distinction of sex.

Article 49

1. If a woman is nursing her child she shall be entitled to interrupt her work for this purpose, under conditions to be prescribed by national laws or regulations.

2. Interruptions of work for the purpose of nursing are to be counted as working hours and remunerated accordingly in cases in which the matter is governed by or in accordance with laws and regulations; in cases in which the matter is governed by collective agreement, the position shall be as determined by the relevant agreement.

Article 50

1. While a woman is absent from work on maternity leave in accordance with the provisions of Article 47, it shall not be lawful for her employer to give her notice of dismissal during such absence, or to give her notice of dismissal at such a time that the notice would expire during such absence.

2. The dismissal of a woman solely because she is pregnant or a nursing mother shall be prohibited.

Table of Ratifications

Brazil*	3/1/65	Mexico	6/20/60
Cuba	12/30/58	Nicaragua	10/1/81
Ecuador	10/3/69	Panama	7/15/71
Guatemala	8/4/61	Philippines	10/10/68
Ivory Coast	5/5/61	Uruguay	6/28/73
Liberia*	7/22/59		

*Indicates the State has denounced the Convention.

Source: International Labour Office, List of Ratifications of Conventions: As at 31 December 1981 (Geneva: International Labour Office, 1982).

14. Convention Concerning Discrimination in Respect of Employment and Occupation

Background

The right to work is clearly stated in Article 23 of the Universal Declaration of Human Rights. Since the Declaration also prohibits discrimination on the basis of sex, this formulation may be seen as an early foundation of this later treaty. This provision is codified in Article 6 of the International Covenant on Economic, Social and Cultural Rights.

The International Labour Organisation put discrimination in employment and occupation on the agenda of its fortieth session (1957) in response to a request from the Commission on Human Rights and the Subcommission on Prevention of Discrimination and Protection of Minorities. Both the Subcommission and the Commission examined drafts of a convention on discrimination in employment and occupation along with comments from governments on the drafts. At its next session on June 15, 1960, the General Conference of the International Labour Organisation adopted the Discrimination (Employment and Occupation) Convention. At the same time they adoted a Recommendation which contained the same basic provisions but in a non-treaty form. The Convention entered into force on June 15, 1960, in accordance with Article 8, twelve months following its ratification by two members.

By this treaty, States Parties obligate themselves to enact national measures to promote equality in employment and occupation; they agree to move towards elimination of discrimination on a number of grounds, including sex. They agree to consult with workers' organizations to this end, to provide educational programs to promote this policy, and to bring laws and administrative practices into compliance with this objective.

Text

Preamble

The General Conference of the International Labour Organisation,

Having been convened at Geneva by the Governing Body of the International Labour Office, and having met in its Forty-second Session on 4 June 1958, and

Having decided upon the adoption of certain proposals with regard to discrimination in the field of employment and occupation, which is the fourth item on the agenda of the session, and

Having determined that these proposals shall take the form of an international Convention, and

Considering that the Declaration of Philadelphia affirms that all human beings, irrespective of race, creed or sex, have the right to pursue both their material well-being and their spiritual development in conditions of freedom and dignity, of economic security and equal opportunity, and

Considering further that discrimination constitutes a violation of rights enunciated by the Universal Declaration of Human Rights,

adopts this twenty-fifth day of the year one thousand nine hundred and fifty-eight the following Convention, which may be cited as the Discrimination (Employment and Occupation) Convention, 1958:

Article 1

1. For the purpose of this Convention the term "discrimination" includes--

   (a) any distinction, exclusion or preference made on the basis of race, colour, sex, religion, political opinion, national extraction or social origin, which has the effect of nullifying or impairing equality of opportunity or treatment in employment or occupation;

(b) such other distinction, exclusion or
    preference which has the effect of
    nullifying or impairing equality of
    opportunity or treatment in employment or
    occupation as may be determined by the
    Member concerned after consultation with
    representative employers' and workers'
    organisations, where such exist, and with
    other appropriate bodies.

2. Any distinction, exclusion or preference in
respect of a particular job based on the inherent
requirements thereof shall not be deemed to be
discrimination.

3. For the purpose of this Convention the terms
"employment" and "occupation" include access to
vocational training, access to employment and to
particular occupations, and terms and conditions of
employment.

Article 2

Each Member for which this Convention is in force
undertakes to declare and pursue a national policy
designed to promote, by methods appropriate to national
conditions and practice, equality of opportunity and
treatment in respect of employment and occupation, with a
view to eliminating any discrimination in respect
thereof.

Article 3

Each member for which this Convention is in force
undertakes, by methods appropriate to national conditions
and practice--

(a) to seek the coperation of employers' and
    workers' organisations and other appropriate
    bodies in promoting the acceptance and
    observance of this policy;

(b) to enact such legislation and to promote
    such educational programmes as may be
    calculated to secure the acceptance and
    observance of the policy;

(c) to repeal any statutory provisions and modify any administrative instructions or practices which are inconsistent with the policy;

(d) to pursue the policy in respect of employment under the direct control of a national authority;

(e) to ensure observance of the policy in the activities of vocational guidance, vocational training and placement services under the direction of a national authority;

(f) to indicate in its annual reports on the application of the the Convention the action taken in pursuance of the policy and the results secured by such action.

Article 4

Any measures affecting an individual who is justifiably suspected of, or engaged in, activities prejudicial to the security of the State shall not be deemed to be discrimination, provided that the individual concerned shall have the right to appeal to a competent body established in accordance with national practice.

Article 5

1. Special measures of protection or assistance provided for in other Conventions or Recommendations adopted by the International Labour conference shall not be deemed to be discrimination.

2. Any Member may, after consultation with representative employers' and workers' organisations, where such exist, determine that other special measures designed to meet the particular requirements of persons who, for reasons such as sex, age, disablement, family responsibilities or social or cultural status, are generally recognised to require special protection or assistance, shall not be deemed to be discrimination.

Article 6

Each Member which ratifies this Convention undertakes to apply it to non-metropolitan territories in accordance with the provisions of the Constitution of the International Labour Organisation.

Article 7

The formal ratifications of this Convention shall be communicated to the Director-General of the International Labour Office for registration.

Article 8

1. This Convention shall be binding only upon those Members of the International Labour Organisation whose ratifications have been registered with the Director-General.

2. It shall come into force twelve months after the date on which the ratifications of two Members have been registered with the Director-General.

3. Thereafter, this Convention shall come into force for any Member twelve months after the date on which its ratification has been registered.

Article 9

1. A Member which has ratified this Convention may denounce it after the expiration of ten years from the date on which the Convention first comes into force, by an act communicated to the Director-General of the International Labour Office for registration. Such denunciation shall not take effect until one year after the date on which it is registered.

2. Each Member which has ratified this Convention and which does not, within the year following the expiration of the period of ten years mentioned in the preceding paragraph, exercise the right of denunciation

provided for in this Article, will be bound for another period of ten years and, thereafter, may denounce this Convention at the expiration of each period of ten years under the terms provided for in this Article.

Article 10

1. The Director-General of the International Labour Office shall notify all Members of the International Labour Organization of the registration of all ratifications and denunciations communicated to him by the Members of the Organisation.

2. When notifying the Members of the Organisation of the registration of the second ratification communicated to him, the Director-General shall draw the attention of the Members of the Organisation to the date upon which the Convention will come into force.

Article 11

The Director-General of the International Labour Office shall communicate to the Secretary-General of the United Nations for registration in accordance with Article 102 of the Charter of the United Nations full particulars of all ratifications and acts of denunciation registered by him in accordance with the provisions of the preceding Articles.

Article 12

At such times as it may consider necessary the Governing Body of the International Labour Office shall present to the General Conference a report on the working of this Convention and shall examine the desirability of placing on the agenda of the Conference the question of its revision in whole or in part.

Article 13

1. Should the Conference adopt a new Convention revising this Convention in whole or in part, then, unless the new Convention otherwise provides--

(a) the ratification by a Member of the new revising Convention shall ipso jure involve the immediate denunciation of this Convention, notwithstanding the provisions of Article 9 above, if and when the new revising Convention shall have come into force;

(b) as from the date when the new revising Convention comes into force this Convention shall cease to be open to ratification by the Members.

2. This Convention shall in any case remain in force in its actual form and content for those Members which have ratified it but have not ratified the revising Convention.

Article 14

The English and French versions of the text of this Convention are equally authoritative.

The foregoing is the authentic text of the Convention duly adopted by the General Conference of the International Labour Organisation during its Forty-second Session which was held at Geneva and declared closed the twenty-sixth day of June 1958.

IN FAITH WHEREOF we have appended our signatures this fifth day of July 1958.

The President of the Conference:
B. K. Das

The Director-General of the International Labour Office:
David A. Morse

Table of Ratifications

Afghanistan	10/1/69	Iraq	6/15/59
Algeria	6/12/69	Israel	1/12/59
Angola	6/4/76	Italy	8/12/63
Argentina	6/18/68	Ivory Coast	5/5/61
Australia	6/15/73	Jamaica	1/10/75
Austria	1/10/73	Jordan	7/4/63
Bangladesh	6/22/27	Kuwait	12/1/66
Barbados	10/14/74	Lebanon	6/1/77
Belgium	3/22/77	Liberia	7/22/59
Benin	5/22/61	Libyan Arab	
Bolivia	1/31/77	Jamahiriya	6/13/61
Brazil	11/26/65	Madagascar	8/11/61
Bulgaria	7/22/60	Malawi	3/22/65
Byelorussian		Mali	3/2/64
SSR	8/4/61	Malta	7/1/68
Canada	11/26/64	Mauritania	11/8/63
Cape Verde	4/3/79	Mexico	9/11/61
Central African		Mongolia	6/3/69
Republic	6/9/64	Morocco	3/27/63
Chad	3/29/66	Mozambique	6/6/77
Chile	9/20/71	Nepal	9/19/74
China	2/13/62	Netherlands	3/15/73
Colombia	3/4/69	Nicaragua	10/31/67
Costa Rica	3/1/62	Niger	3/23/62
Cuba	8/26/65	Nigeria	9/24/59
Cyprus	2/2/68	Pakistan	1/24/61
Czechoslovakia	1/21/64	Panama	5/16/66
Denmark	6/22/60	Paraguay	7/10/67
Dominican		Peru	8/10/70
Republic	7/13/64	Philippines	11/17/60
Ecuador	7/10/62	Poland	5/30/61
Egypt (U. A. R.)	5/10/60	Portugal	11/19/59
Ethiopia	6/11/66	Qatar	8/18/76
Finland	4/23/70	Romania	6/6/73
France	5/28/81	Rwanda	2/2/81
Gabon	5/29/61	Saudi Arabia	6/15/78
German Democratic		Senegal	11/13/67
Republic	5/7/75	Sierra Leone	10/14/66
Germany, Federal		Somalia	12/8/61
Republic of	6/15/61	Spain	11/6/67
Ghana	4/4/61	Sudan	10/22/70
Guatemala	10/11/60	Swaziland	6/5/81
Guinea	9/1/60	Sweden	6/20/62
Guinea-Bissau	2/21/77	Switzerland	7/13/61
Guyana	6/13/75	Syrian Arab	
Haiti	11/9/76	Republic (Syria)	5/10/60
Honduras	6/20/60	Trinidad and	
Hungary	6/20/61	Tobago	11/26/70
Iceland	7/29/63	Tunisia	9/14/59
India	6/3/60	Turkey	7/19/67
Iran	6/30/64	Ukrainian SSR	8/4/61

```
Union of Soviet              Viet Nam          1/6/64
  Socialist                  Yemen             8/22/69
  Republics       5/4/61     Yugoslavia        2/2/61
Upper Volta       4/16/62    Zambia            10/23/79
Venezuela         6/3/71
```

Source: International   Labour   Office,   List   of
Ratifications of Conventions: As   at 31 December 1981
(Geneva: International Labour Office, 1982).

15. Convention Against Discrimination in Education

Background

In 1958 the General Conference of the United Nations Educational, Scientific and Cultural Organization decided to draft an international convention on a number of issues related to discrimination in education. The Conference asked the Director-General to draft a treaty and circulate it to Member States for suggestions and revisions. The revised draft was adopted by the General Conference on December 14, 1960. The Conference also adopted a Recommendation, which was basically identical to the treaty but was not in treaty form and not legally binding. The Economic and Social Council noted the Convention and Recommendation with approval on July 18, 1961, in resolution 821 VB (XXXII). The General Conference of the United Nations Educational, Scientific and Cultural Organization on December 10, 1962, adopted the Protocol Instituting a Conciliation and Good Offices Commission for the purpose of settling disputes arising under the terms of the Convention. The Convention came into force on May 22, 1962, in accordance with Article 14, three months after the deposit of the third instrument of ratification. The Protocol came into force on October 24, 1968, in accordance with Article 24, three months after the deposit of the fifteenth instrument of ratification.

The Convention prohibits educational discrimination on a number of bases. It calls on the States Parties to eliminate discrimination in various phases of education: administration of schools; admission of students; financial aid; public assistance; facilities; and teacher qualifications. The objective is equality of opportunity as well as treatment and States are asked to take all appropriate steps to achieve this goal.

Text

Preamble

The General Conference of the United Nations Educational, Scientific and Cultural Organization, meeting in Paris from 14 November to 15 December 1960, at its eleventh session,

Recalling that the Universal Declaration of Human Rights asserts the principle of non-discrimination and proclaims that every person has the right to education,

Considering that, under the terms of its Constitution, the United Nations Educational, Scientific and Cultural Organization has the purpose of instituting collaboration among the nations with a view to furthering for all universal respect for human rights and equality of educational opportunity,

Recognizing that, consequently, the United Nations Educational, Scientific and Cultural Organization, while respecting the diversity of national educational systems, has the duty not only to proscribe any form of discrimination in education but also to promote equality of opportunity and treatment for all in education,

Having before it proposals concerning the different aspects of discrimination in education, constituting item 17.1.4 of the agenda of the session,

Having decided at its tenth session that this question should be made the subject of an international convention as well as of recommendations to Member States,

Adopts this Convention on the fourteenth day of December 1960

Article 1

1. For the purposes of this Convention, the term "discrimination" includes any distinction, exclusion, limitation or preference which, being based on race, colour, sex, language, religion, political or other opinion, national or social origin, economic condition or birth, has the purpose or effect of nullifying or impairing equality of treatment in education and in particular:

(a) Of depriving any person or group of persons
    of access to education of any type or at any
    level;

(b) Of limiting any person or group of persons
    to education of an inferior standard;

(c) Subject to the provisions of Article 2 of
    this Convention, of establishing or
    maintaining separate educational systems or
    institutions for persons or groups of
    persons; or

(d) Of inflicting on any person or group of
    persons conditions which are incompatible
    with the dignity of man.

2. For the purposes of this Convention, the term
"education" refers to all types and levels of education,
and includes access to education, the standard and
quality of education, and the conditions under which it
is given.

Article 2

When permitted in a State, the following situations
shall not be deemed to constitute discrimination, within
the meaning of Article 1 of this Convention:

(a) The establishment or maintenance of separate
    educational systems or institutions for
    pupils of the two sexes, if these systems or
    institutions offer equivalent access to
    education, provide a teaching staff with
    qualifications of the same standard as well
    as school premises and equipment of the same
    quality, and afford the opportunity to take
    the same or equivalent courses of study;

(b) The establishment or maintenance, for
    religious or linguistic reasons, of separate
    educational systems or institutions offering
    an education which is in keeping with the
    wishes of the pupil's parents or legal
    guardians, if participation in such systems
    or attendance at such institutions is
    optional and if the education provided
    conforms to such standards as may be laid

down or approved by the competent authorities, in particular for education of the same level;

(c) The establishment or maintenance of private educational institutions, if the object of the institutions is not to secure the exclusion of any group but to provide educational facilities in addition to those provided by the public authorities, if the institutions are conducted in accordance with that object, and if the education provided conforms with such standards as may be laid down or approved by the competent authorities, in particular for education of the same level.

Article 3

In order to eliminate and prevent discrimination within the meaning of this Convention, the States Parties thereto undertake:

(a) To abrogate any statutory provisions and any administrative instructions and to discontinue any administrative practices which involve discrimination in education;

(b) To ensure, by legislation where necessary, that there is no discrimination in the admission of pupils to educational institutions;

(c) Not to allow any differences of treatment by the public authorities between nationals, except on the basis of merit or need, in the matter of school fees and the grant of scholarships or other forms of assistance to pupils and necessary permits and facilities for the pursuit of studies in foreign countries;

(d) Not to allow, in any form of assistance granted by the public authorities to educational institutions, any restrictions or preference based solely on the ground that pupils belong to a particular group;

(e) To give foreign nationals resident within their territory the same access to education as that given to their own nationals.

Article 4

The States Parties to this Convention undertake furthermore to formulate, develop and apply a national policy which, by methods appropriate to the circumstances and to national usage, will tend to promote equality of opportunity and of treatment in the matter of education and in particular:

(a) To make primary education free and compulsory; make secondary education in its different forms generally available and accessible to all; make higher education equally accessible to all on the basis of individual capacity; assure compliance by all with the obligation to attend school prescribed by law;

(b) To ensure that the standards of education are equivalent in all public educational institutions of the same level, and that the conditions relating to the quality of the educatin provided are also equivalent;

(c) To encourage and intensify by appropriate methods the education of persons who have not received any primary education or who have not completed the entire primary education course and the continuation of their education on the basis of individual capacity;

(d) To provide training for the teaching profession without discrimination.

Article 5

1. The States Parties to this Convention agree that:

(a) Education shall be directed to the full development of the human personality and to the strengthening of respect for human rights and fundamental freedoms; it shall promote understanding, tolerance and friendship among all nations, racial or religious groups, and shall further the activities of the United Nations for the maintenance of peace;

(b) It is essential to respect the liberty of parents and, where applicable, of legal guardians, firstly to choose for their children institutions other than those maintained by the public authorities but conforming to such minimum educational standards as may be laid down or aproved by the competent authorities and, secondly, to ensure in a manner consistent with the procedures followed in the State for the application of its legislation, the religious and moral education of the children in conformity with their own convictions; and no person or group of persons should be compelled to receive religious instruction inconsistent with his or their conviction;

(c) It is essential to recognize the right of members of national minorities to carry on their own educational activities, including the maintenance of schools and, depending on the educational policy of each State, the use or the teaching of their own language, provided however:

(i) That this right is not exercised in a manner which prevents the members of these minorities from understanding the culture and language of the community as a whole and from participating in its activities, or which prejudices national sovereignty;

(ii) That the standard of education is not lower than the general standard laid down or approved by the competent authorities; and

(iii) That attendance at such schools is optional.

2. The State Parties to this Convention undertake to take all necessary measures to ensure the application

of the principles enunciated in paragraph 1 of this Article.

Article 6

In the application of this Convention, the States Parties to it undertake to pay the greatest attention to any recommendations hereafter adopted by the General Conference of the United Nations Educational, Scientific and Cultural Organization defining the measures to be taken against the different forms of discrimination in education and for the purpose of ensuring equality of opportunity and treatment in education.

Article 7

The States Parties to this Convention shall in their own periodic reports submitted to the General Conference of the United Nations Educational, Scientific and Cultural Organization on dates and in a manner to be determined by it, give information on the legislative and administrative provisions which they have adopted and other action which they have taken for the application of this Convention, including that taken for the formulation and the development of the national policy defined in Article 4 as well as the results achieved and the obstacles encountered in the application of that policy.

Article 8

Any dispute which may arise between any two or more States Parties to this Convention concerning the interpretation or application of this Convention, which is not settled by negotiation shall at the request of the parties to the dispute be referred, failing other means of settling the dispute, to the International Court of Justice for decision.

Article 9

Reservations to this Convention shall not be permitted.

Article 10

This Convention shall not have the effect of diminishing the rights which individuals or groups may enjoy by virtue of agreements concluded between two or more States, where such rights are not contrary to the letter or spirit of this Convention.

Article 11

This Convention is drawn up in English, French, Russian and Spanish, the four texts being equally authoritative.

Article 12

1. This Convention shall be subject to ratification or acceptance by States Members of the United Nations Educational, Scientific and Cultural Organization in accordance with their respective constitutional procedures.

2. The instruments of ratification or acceptance shall be deposited with the Director-General of the United Nations Educational, Scientific and Cultural Organization.

Article 13

1. This Convention shall be open to accession by all States not Members of the United Nations Educational, Scientific and Cultural Organizations which are invited to do so by the Executive Board of the Organization.

2. Accession shall be effected by the deposit of an instrument of accession with the Director-General of the United Nations Educational, Scientific and Cultural Organization.

Article 14

This Convention shall enter into force three months after the date of the deposit of the third instrument of ratification, acceptance or accession, but only with respect to those States which have deposited their respective instruments on or before that date. It shall enter into force with respect to any other State three months after the deposit of its instrument of ratification, acceptance or accession.

Article 15

The States Parties to this Convention recognize that the Convention is applicable not only to their metropolitan territory but also to all non-self-governing, trust, colonial and other territories for the international relations of which they are responsible; they undertake to consult, if necessary, the governments or other competent authorities of these territories on or before ratification, acceptance or accession with a view to securing the application of the Convention to those territories, and to notify the Director-General of the United Nations Educational, Scientific and Cultural Organization of the territories to which it is accordingly applied, the notification to take effect three months after the date of its receipt.

Article 16

1. Each State Party to this Convention may denounce the Convention on its own behalf or on behalf of any territory for whose international relations it is responsible.

2. The denunciation shall be notified by an instrument in writing, deposited with the Director-General of the United Nations Educational, Scientific and Cultural Organization.

3. The denunciation shall take effect twelve months after the receipt of the instrument of denunciation.

Article 17

The Director-General of the United Nations Educational, Scientific and Cultural Organization shall inform the States Members of the Organization, the States not members of the Organization which are referred to in Article 13, as well as the United Nations, of the deposit of all the instruments of ratification, acceptance and accession provided for in Articles 12 and 13, and of the notifications and denunciations provided for in Articles 15 and 16 respectively.

Article 18

1. This Convention may be revised by the General Conference of the United Nations Educational, Scientific and Cultural Organization. Any such revision shall, however, bind only the States which shall become Parties to the revising convention.

2. If the General Conference should adopt a new convention revising this Convention in whole or in part, then, unless the new convention otherwise provides, this Convention shall cease to be open to ratification, acceptance or accession as from the date on which the new revising convention enters into force.

Article 19

In conformity with Artical 102 of the Charter of the United Nations, this Convention shall be registered with the Secretariat of the United Nations at the request of the Director-General of the United Nations Educational, Scientific and Cultural Organization.

DONE in Paris, this fifteenth day of December 1960, in two authentic copies bearing the signatures of the President of the eleventh session of the General Conference and of the Director-General of the United Nations Educational, Scientific and Cultural

Organization, which shall be deposited in the archives of the United Nations Educational, Scientific and Cultural Organization, and certified true copies of which shall be delivered to all the States referred to in Articles 12 and 13 as well as to the United Nations.

The foregoing is the authentic text of the Convention duly adopted by the General Conference of the United Nations Educational, Scientific and Cultural Organization during its eleventh session, which was held in Paris and declared closed the fifteenth day of December 1960.

IN FAITH WHEREOF we have appended our signatures this fifteenth day of December 1960.

The President of the General Conference:
Akale-Work Abte-Wold

The Director-General:
Vittorino Veronese

Table of Ratifications

Albania	11/21/63	Germany, Federal	
Algeria	12/24/68	Republic of	7/17/68
Argentina	10/30/73	Guinea	12/11/64
Australia	11/29/66	Hungary	1/16/64
Barbados	6/24/75	Indonesia	1/10/67
Benin	7/9/63	Iran	7/17/68
Brazil	4/19/68	Iraq*	6/28/77
Bulgaria	12/4/62	Israel	9/2/61
Byelorussian		Italy	10/6/66
SSR	12/12/62	Jordan	4/6/76
Central African		Kuwait	1/15/63
Republic	2/22/62	Lebanon	10/27/64
Chile	10/26/71	Liberia	5/17/62
China	2/12/65	Libyan Arab	
Congo	9/16/68	Jamahiriya	1/9/73
Costa Rica	9/10/63	Luxembourg	1/20/70
Cuba	11/2/62	Madagascar	12/21/64
Cyprus	6/9/70	Malta	1/6/66
Czechoslovakia	3/14/63	Mauritius	8/20/70
Denmark*	9/4/63	Mongolia	11/4/64
Dominican		Morocco	8/30/68
Republic	8/30/77	Netherlands	3/25/66
Ecuador	3/5/79	New Zealand	2/12/63
Egypt (U. A. R.)	3/28/62	Niger	9/16/68
Finland	10/18/51	Nigeria	11/18/69
France	9/11/61	Norway	1/8/63
German Democratic		Panama	8/10/67
Republic	7/5/73	Peru	12/19/66

Philippines	11/19/64	Union of Soviet	
Poland	9/15/64	Socialist	
Romania	7/9/64	Republics	8/1/62
Saudi Arabia	8/17/73	United Kingdom of	
Senegal	9/25/67	Great Britain	
Sierra Leone	6/2/67	and N.Ireland*	3/14/62
Spain	8/20/69	United Republic	
Swaziland	10/8/70	of Tanzania	1/9/79
Sweden	3/21/68	Venezuela	12/16/68
Tunisia	8/29/69	Viet Nam	6/12/68
Uganda	9/9/68	Yugoslavia	10/14/64
Ukrainian SSR	12/19/62		

*Indicates reservation or declaration at time of ratification.

Source: United Nations Educational, Scientific and Cultural Organization, UNESCO's Standard-Setting Instruments, (Paris: United Nations Educational, Scientific and Cultural Organization, 1981).

16. Convention on Consent to Marriage, Minimum Age for Marriage, and Registration of Marriages

Background

The basic need for a treaty on this subject was identified in 1956 by the Conference of Plenipotentiaries convened by the Economic and Social Council to prepare the Supplementary Convention on the Abolition of Slavery, the Slave Trade, and Institutions and Practices Similar to Slavery. The Conference suggested that the Economic and Social Council initiate a study of marriage law drawing attention to the desirability of free consent of the partners and of setting a minimum age. In 1957 the Council referred the isssue to the Commission on the Status of Women. A draft treaty was presented by the Commission to the Council and it was adopted by the General Assembly in Resolution 1763 (XVII) on November 7, 1962, by a vote of 92 to 0 with 7 abstentions.

In order to ensure free consent of the parties to a marriage, the treaty requires that following public announcement of the marriage, the parties must give personal consent in the presence of a competent authority. It also requires States to legislate a minimum age for marriage and to set up a program of official registration of marriages.

Text

Preamble

The Contracting States,

Desiring, in conformity with the Charter of the United Nations, to promote universal respect for, and observance of, human rights and fundamental freedoms for all, without distinction as to race, sex, language or religion,

- 177 -

Recalling that article 16 of the Universal Declaration of Human Rights states that:

"(1) Men and women of full age, without any limitation due to race, nationality or religion, have the right to marry and to found a family. They are entitled to equal rights as to marriage, during marriage and at its dissolution.

"(2) Marriage shall be entered into only with the free and full consent of the intending spouses.",

Recalling further that the General Assembly of the United Nations declared, by resolution 843 (IX) of 17 December 1954, that certain customs, ancient laws and practices relating to marriage and the family were inconsistent with the principles set forth in the Charter of the United Nations and in the Universal Declaration of Human Rights,

Reaffirming that all States, including those which have or assume responsibility for the administration of Non-Self-Governing and Trust Territories until their achievement of independence, should take all appropriate measures with a view to abolishing such customs, ancient laws and practices by ensuring, inter alia, complete freedom in the choice of a spouse, eliminating completely child marriages and the betrothal of young girls before the age of puberty, establishing appropriate penalties where necessary and establishing a civil or other register in which all marriages will be recorded,

Hereby Agree as hereinafter provided:

Article 1

1. No marriage shall be legally entered into without the full and free consent of both parties, such consent to be expressed by them in person after due publicity and in the presence of the authority competent to solemnize the marriage and of witnesses, as prescribed by law.

2. Notwithstanding anything in paragraph 1 above, it shall not be necessary for one of the parties to be present when the competent authority is satisfied that the circumstances are exceptional and that the party has,

before a competent authority and in such manner as may be prescribed by law, expressed and not withdrawn consent.

Article 2

States parties to the present Convention shall take legislative action to specify a minimum age for marriage. No marriage shall be legally entered into by any person under this age, except where a competent authority has granted a dispensation as to age, for serious reasons, in the interest of the intending spouses.

Article 3

All marriages shall be registered in an appropriate offical register by the competent authority.

Article 4

1. The present Convention shall, until 31 December 1963, be open for signature on behalf of all States Members of the United Nations or members of any of the specialized agencies, and of any other State invited by the General Assembly of the United Nations to become party to the Convention.

2. The present Convention is subject to ratification. The instruments of ratification shall be deposited with the Secretary-General of the United Nations.

Article 5

1. The present Convention shall be open for accession to all States referred to in article 4, paragraph 1.

2. Accession shall be effected by the deposit of an instrument of accession with the Secretary-General of the United Nations.

Article 6

1. The present Convention shall come into force on the ninetieth day following the date of deposit of the eighth instrument of ratification or accession.

2. For each State ratifying or acceding to the Convention after the deposit of the eighth instrument of ratification or accession, the Convention shall enter into force on the ninetieth day after deposit by such State of its instrument of ratification or accession.

Article 7

1. Any Contracting State may denounce the present Convention by written notification to the Secretary-General of the United-Nations. Denunciation shall take effect one year after the date of receipt of the notification by the Secretary-General.

2. The present Convention shall cease to be in force as from the date when the denunciation which reduces the number of parties to less than eight becomes effective.

Article 8

Any dispute which may arise between any two or more Contracting States concerning the interpretation or application of the present Convention which is not settled by negotiation shall, at the request of all the parties to the dispute, be referred to the International Court of Justice for decision, unless the parties agree to another mode of settlement.

Article 9

The Secretary-General of the United Nations shall notify all States Members of the United Nations and the non-member States contemplated in article 4, paragraph 1, of the present Convention of the following:

(a) Signatures and instruments of ratification received in accordance with article 4;

(b) Instruments of accession received in accordance with article 5;

(c) The date upon which the Convention enters into force in accordance with article 6;

(d) Notifications of denunciation received in accordance with article 7, paragraph 1.

(e) Abrogation in accordance with article 7 paragraph 2.

Article 10

1. The present Convention, of which the Chinese, English, French, Russian and Spanish texts shall be equally authentic, shall be deposited in the archives of the United Nations.

2. The Secretary-General of the United Nations shall transmit a certified copy of the Convention to all States Members of the United Nations and to the non-member States contemplated in article 4, paragraph 1.

IN FAITH WHEREOF the undersigned, being duly authorized, have signed, on behalf of their respective Governments, the present Convention which was opened for signature at the Headquarters of the United Nations, New York, on the tenth day of December, one thousand nine hundred and sixty-two.

Table of Ratifications

Argentina	2/26/70	Finland*	8/18/64
Austria	10/1/69	France+	12/10/62
Barbados	10/1/79	German Democratic	
Benin	10/19/65	Republic	7/16/74
Brazil	2/11/70	Germany, Federal	
Chile+	12/10/62	Republic of	7/9/69
China+	4/4/63	Greece+*	1/3/63
Cuba	8/20/65	Guinea	1/24/78
Czechoslovakia	3/5/65	Hungary*	11/5/75
Denmark*	9/8/64	Iceland*	10/18/77
Dominican		Israel+	12/10/62
Republic*	10/8/64	Italy+	12/20/63
Fiji*	7/19/71	Mali	8/19/64

Netherlands*	7/2/65	Trinidad and	
New Zealand	6/12/64	Tobago	10/2/69
Niger	12/1/64	Tunisia	1/24/68
Norway*	9/10/64	United Kingdom of	
Philippines*	1/21/65	Great Britain	
Poland	1/8/65	and N.Ireland*	7/9/70
Romania+	12/27/63	United States of	
Samoa	8/24/64	America+*	12/10/62
Spain	4/15/69	Upper Volta	12/8/64
Sri Lanka+	12/12/62	Yugoslavia	6/19/64
Sweden*	6/16/64		

+Indicates signature only.

*Indicates reservation or declaration at time of signature or ratification. Most of these reservations were to Article 1 paragraph 2 which with certain conditions, allows proxy marriage.

Source: United Nations, Multilateral Treaties Deposited with the Secretary-General: Status as at 31 December 1981 (New York: United Nations, 1982).

17. The International Covenants on Human Rights: Covenant and Political Rights

Background

These treaties were drafted by the Commission on Human Rights. The Commission originally planned to draft one treaty as a second step in the process of developing an international bill of rights; they hoped to translate the Universal Declaration of Human Rights into a single treaty which would specify and codify the principles set forth in the Declaration. After much study and debate, however, it was decided that two treaties should be drafted, one on civil and political rights which would be immediately binding and a second on economic, social and cultural rights, which would obligate States to take steps to progressively achieve the rights set forth therein. The Covenants were submitted, by the Commission, to the Third Committee (Social, Cultural and Humanitarian) in 1954, and were adopted unanimously by the General Assembly in Resolution 2200 (XXI) on December 16, 1966. The Civil and Political Rights Covenant came into force on March 23, 1976, in accordance with Article 49, three months following the deposition of the thirty-fifth instrument of ratification. The Economic, Social and Cultural Rights Covenant came into force January 3, 1976, in accordance with Article 27, three months after the deposit of the thirty-fifth instrument of ratification.

Text (Excerpts)

Preamble

The State Parties to the Present Covenant,

Considering that, in accordance with the principles proclaimed in the Charter of the United Nations, recognition of the inherent dignity and of the equal and inalienable rights of all members of the human family is the foundation of freedom, justice and peace in the world,

Recognizing that these rights derive from the inherent dignity of the of the human person,

Recognizing that, in accordance with the Universal Declaration of Human Rights, the ideal of free human beings enjoying civil and political freedom and freedom from fear and want can only be achieved if conditions are created whereby everyone may enjoy his civil and political rights, as well as his economic, social and cultural rights,

Considering the obligation of States under the Charter of the United Nations to promote universal respect for, and observance of, human rights and freedoms,

Realizing that the individual, having duties to other individuals and to the community to which he belongs, is under a responsibility to strive for the promotion and observance of the rights recognized in the present Covenant,

Agree upon the following articles:

* * * * *

PART II

Article 2

1. Each State Pary to the present Covenant undertakes to respect and to ensure to all individuals within its territory and subject to its jurisdiction the rights recognized in the present Covenant, without distinction of any kind, such as race, colour, sex, language, religion, political or other opinion, national or social origin, property, birth or other status.

2. Where not already provided for by existing legislative or other measures, each State Party to the present Covenant undertakes to take the necessary steps,

in accordance with its constitutional processes and with the provisions of the present Covenant, to adopt such legislative or other measures as may be necessary to give effect to the rights recognized in the present Covenant.

3. Each State Party to the present Covenant undertakes:

(a) To ensure that any person whose rights or freedoms as herein recognized are violated shall have an effective remedy, notwithstanding that the violation has been committed by persons acting in an official capacity;

(b) To ensure that any person claiming such a remedy shall have his right thereto determined by competent judicial, administrative or legislative authorities, or by any other competent authority provided for by the legal system of the State, and to develop the possibilities of judicial remedy;

(c) To ensure that the competent authorities shall enforce such remedies when granted.

Article 3

The States Parties to the present Covenant undertake to ensure the equal right of men and women to the enjoyment of all civil and political rights set forth in the present Covenant.

* * * * *

Article 6

1. Every human being has the inherent right to life. This right shall be protected by law. No one shall be arbitrarily deprived of his life.

* * * * *

5. Sentence of death shall not be imposed for crimes committed by persons below eighteen years of age and shall not be carried out on pregnant women.

* * * * *

Article 23

1. The family is the natural and fundamental group unit of society and is entitled to protection by society and the State.

2. The right of men and women of marriageable as to marry and to found a family shall be recognized.

3. No marriage shall be entered into without the full and free consent of the intending spouses.

4. States Parties to the present Covenant shall take appropriate steps to ensure equality of rights and responsibilities of spouses as to marriage, during marriage and at its dissolution. In the case of dissolution, provision shall be made for the necessary protection of any children.

Article 24

1. Every child shall have, without any discrimination as to race, colour, sex, language, religion, national or social origin, property or birth, the right to such measures of protection as are required by his status as a minor, on the part of his family, society and the State.

* * * * *

Article 25

Every citizen shall have the right and the opportunity, without any of the distinctions mentioned in article 2 and without unreasonable restrictions:

(a) To take part in the conduct of public affairs, directly or through freely chosen representatiaves;

(b) To vote and to be elected at genuine periodic elections which shall be by universal and equal suffrage and shall be held by secret ballot, guaranteeing the free expression of the will of the electors;

(c) To have access, on general terms of equality, to public service in his country.

Article 26

All persons are equal before the law and are entitled without any discrimination to the equal protection of the law. In this respect, the law shall prohibit any discrimination and guarantee to all persons equal and effective protection against discrimination on any ground such as race, colour, sex, language, religion, political or other opinion, national or social origin, property, birth or other status.

*   *   *   *   *

Table of Ratifications

Algeria+	12/10/68	Democratic	
Argentina	2/19/68	People's Rep.	
Australia*	8/13/80	of Korea	9/14/81
Austria*	9/10/78	Denmark*	1/6/72
Barbados*	1/5/73	Dominican	
Belgium+	12/10/68	Republic	1/4/78
Bulgaria*	9/21/70	Ecuador	3/6/69
Byelorussian		Egypt (U. A. R.)+	8/4/67
SSR*	11/12/73	El Salvador	11/30/79
Canada	5/19/76	Finland*	8/19/75
Central African		France*	11/4/80
Republic	5/8/81	Gambia*	3/22/79
Chile*	2/10/72	German Democratic	
China+	10/5/67	Republic*	11/8/73
Colombia*	10/29/69	Germany, Federal	
Costa Rica	11/29/68	Republic of*	12/17/73
Cyprus	4/2/69	Guinea*	1/24/78
Czechoslovakia*	12/23/65	Guyana*	2/15/77
Democratic		Honduras+	12/19/66
Kampuchea+	10/17/80	Hungary*	1/17/74

- 187 -

Iceland*	8/22/79	Portugal	6/15/78
India*	4/10/79	Romania*	12/9/74
Iran	6/24/75	Rwanda	4/16/75
Iraq*	1/25/71	Saint Vincent and	
Ireland+	10/1/73	the Grenadines	11/9/81
Israel+	12/19/66	Senegal	2/13/78
Italy*	9/15/78	Spain	4/27/77
Jamaica	10/3/75	Sri Lanka	6/11/80
Japan*	6/21/79	Suriname	12/28/76
Jordan	5/28/75	Sweden*	12/6/71
Kenya	5/1/72	Syrian Arab	
Lebanon	11/3/72	Republic *	4/21/69
Liberia+	4/18/67	Trinidad and	
Libyan Arab		Tobago*	12/21/78
Jamahiriya*	5/15/70	Tunisia	3/18/69
Luxembourg+	11/26/74	Ukrainian SSR*	11/12/73
Madagascar	6/21/71	Union of Soviet	
Mali	7/16/74	Socialist	
Mauritius	12/12/73	Republics*	10/16/73
Mexico*	3/23/81	United Kingdom of	
Mongolia*	11/18/74	Great Britain	
Morocco	5/3/79	and N. Ireland*	5/20/76
Netherlands*	12/11/78	United Republic	
New Zealand*	12/28/78	of Tanzania	6/11/76
Nicaragua*	3/12/80	United States of	
Norway*	9/13/72	America+	10/5/77
Panama	3/8/77	Uruguay*	4/1/70
Peru	4/28/78	Venezuela*	5/10/78
Philippines+	12/19/66	Yugoslavia	6/2/71
Poland	3/18/77	Zaire	11/1/76

+Indicates signature only.

*Indicates reservation or declaration at time of signature or ratification.

Source: United Nations, Multilateral Treaties Deposited with the Secretary-General: Status as at 31 December 1981 (New York: United Nations, 1982).

18. The International Covenants on Human Rights: Covenant on Economic, Social and Cultural Rights

Preamble

The States Parties to the present Covenant,

Considering that, in accordance with the principles proclaimed in the Charter of the United Nations, recognition of the inherent dignity and of the equal and inalienable rights of all members of the human family is the foundation of freedom, justice and peace in the world.

Recognizing that these rights derive from the inherent dignity of human person.

Recognizing that, in accordance with the Universal Declaration of Human Rights, the ideal of free human beings enjoying freedom from fear and want can only be achieved if conditions are created whereby everyone may enjoy his economic, social and cultural rights, as well as his civil and political rights,

Considering the obligation of States under the Charter of the United Nations to promote universal respect for, and observance of, human rights and freedoms,

Realizing that the individual, having duties to other individuals and to the community to which he belongs, is under a responsibility to strive for the promotion and observance of the rights recognized in the present Covenant,

Agree upon the following articles:

* * * * *

Article 2

*　*　*　*　*

2. The States Parties to the present Covenant undertake to guarantee that the rights enunciated in the present Covenant will be exercised without discrimination of any kind as to race, colour, sex, language, religion, political or other opinion, national or social origin, property, birth or other status.

Article 3

The States Parties to the present Covenant undertake to ensure the equal right of men and women to the enjoyment of all economic, social and cultural rights set forth in the present Covenant.

Article 4

The States Parties to the present Covenant recognize that, in the enjoyment of those rights provided by the State in conformity with the present Covenant, the State may subject such rights only to such limitations as are determined by law only in so far as this may be compatible with the nature of these rights and solely for the purpose of promoting the general welfare in a democratic society.

Article 5

1. Nothing in the present Covenant may be interpreted as implying for any State, group or person any right to engage in any activity or to perform any act aimed at the destruction of any rights or freedoms recognized herein, or at their limitation to the greater extent than is provided for in the present Covenant.

2. No restriction upon or derogation from any of the fundamental human rights recognized or existing in any country in virtue of law, conventions, regulations or

custom shall be admitted on the pretext that the present Covenant does not recognize such rights or that it recognizes them to a lesser extent.

*   *   *   *   *

Article 7

The States Parties to the present Covenant recognize the right of everyone to the enjoyment of just and favourable conditions of work, which ensure in particular:

(a) Remuneration which provides all workers, as a mimimum with:

(i) Fair wages and equal remuneration for work of equal value without distinction of any kind, in particular women being guaranteed conditions of work not inferior to those enjoyed by men, with equal pay for equal work;

(ii) A decent living for themselves and their families in accordance with the provisions of the present Convenant;

(b) Safe and healthy working conditions;

(c) Equal opportunity for everyone to be promoted in his employment to an appropriate higher level, subject to no considerations other than those of seniority and competence;

*   *   *   *   *

Article 10

The States Parties to the present Covenant recognize that:

1. The widest possible protection and assistance should be accorded to the family,

which is the natural and fundamental group
unit of society, particularly for its
establishment and while it is responsible
for the care and education of dependent
children. Marriage must be entered into
with the free consent of the intending
spouses.

2. Special protection should be accorded to
mothers during a reasonable period before
and after childbirth. During such period
working mothers should be accorded paid
leave or leave with adequate social security
benefits.

Table of Ratifications

Algeria+	12/10/68	Germany, Federal	
Argentina+	2/19/68	Republic of	12/17/73
Australia	12/10/75	Guinea*	1/24/78
Austria	9/10/78	Guyana	2/15/77
Barbados*	1/5/73	Honduras	2/17/81
Belgium+	12/10/68	Hungary*	1/17/74
Bulgaria*	9/21/70	Iceland	8/22/79
Byelorussian		India*	4/10/79
SSR*	11/12/73	Iran	6/24/75
Canada	5/19/76	Iraq*	1/25/71
Central African		Ireland+	10/1/73
Republic	5/8/81	Israel+	12/19/66
Chile	2/10/72	Italy	9/15/78
China+	10/5/67	Jamaica	10/3/75
Columbia	10/29/69	Japan*	6/21/79
Costa Rica	11/29/68	Jordan	5/28/75
Cyprus	4/2/69	Kenya*	5/1/72
Czechoslovakia*	12/23/75	Lebanon	11/3/72
Democratic		Liberia+	4/18/67
Kampuchea+	10/17/80	Libyan Arab	
Democratic		Jamahiriya*	5/15/70
People's Republic		Luxembourg+	11/26/74
of Korea+	9/14/81	Madagascar*	9/22/71
Denmark*	1/6/72	Mali	7/16/74
Dominican		Malta+*	10/22/68
Republic	1/4/78	Mauritius	12/12/73
Ecuador	3/6/69	Mexico*	3/23/81
Egypt*	8/4/67	Mongolia*	11/18/74
El Salvador	11/30/79	Morocco	5/3/79
Finland	8/19/75	Netherlands*	12/11/78
France*	11/4/80	New Zealand*	12/28/78
Gambia	12/29/78	Nicaragua	3/12/80
German Democratic		Norway*	9/13/72
Republic*	11/8/73	Panama	3/8/77
		Peru	4/28/78

- 192 -

Philippines	6/7/74	Tunisia	3/18/69
Poland	3/18/77	Ukrainian SSR*	11/12/73
Portugal	7/31/78	Union of Soviet	
Romania*	12/9/74	Socialist	
Rwanda*	4/16/75	Republics*	10/16/73
Saint Vincent and		United Kingdom of	
the Grenadines	11/9/81	Great Britain	
Senegal	2/13/78	and N.Ireland*	5/20/76
Spain	4/27/77	United Republic	
Sri Lanka	6/11/80	of Tanzania	6/11/76
Suriname	12/28/76	United States of	
Sweden*	12/6/71	America+	10/5/77
Syrian Arab		Uruguay	4/1/70
Republic *	4/21/69	Venezuela	5/10/78
Trinidad and		Yugoslavia	6/2/71
Tobago*	12/8/78	Zaire	11/1/76

+Indicates signature only.

*Indicates reservation or declaration at time of signature or ratification.

Source: United Nations, Multilateral Treaties Deposited with the Secretary-General: Status as at 31 December 1981 (New York: United Nations, 1982).

19. Declaration on the Elimination of Discrimination Against Women

Background

This Declaration was drafted by the Commission on the Status of Women in response to a request by the General Assembly. The Commission received proposals from Member States, specialized agencies, and nongovernmental organizations. In 1966 a draft was submitted to Member States for comment; this draft was then revised, adopted by the Commission in 1967, and considered by the Third Committee the same year. The Third Committee (Social, Cultural and Humanitarian) made some amendments and on November 7, 1967, the General Assembly unanimously adopted the Declaration in Resolution 2263 (XXII). The Declaration sets forth as its basic objective the elimination of discrimination based on sex. It consolidates fundamental principles found in other basic documents, including the United Nations Charter, the Universal Declaration of Human Rights, and the International Covenants on Human Rights. It reaffirms the need to advance the status of women in family life, social, political, economic, and cultural affairs, at the national and international level. It is designed to clearly enunciate basic principles; as a resolution of the General Assembly it is not, in itself, a legally binding instrument.

Text

The General Assembly,

Considering that the peoples of the United Nations have, in the Charter, reaffirmed their faith in fundamental human rights, in the dignity and worth of the human person and in the equal rights of men and women,

Considering that the Universal Declaration on Human Rights asserts the principle of non-discrimination and proclaims that all human beings are born free and equal in dignity and rights and that everyone is entitled to all the rights and freedoms set forth therin without distinction of any kind, including any distinction as to sex,

Taking into account the resolutions, declarations, conventions and recommendations of the United Nations and the specialized agencies designed to eliminate all forms of discrimination and to promote equal rights for men and women,

Concerned that, despite the Charter of the United Nations, the Universal Declaration of Human Rights, the International Covenants on Human Rights and other instruments of the United Nations and the specialized agencies and despite the progress made in the matter of equality of rights, there continues to exist considerable discrimination against women,

Considering that discrimination against women is incompatible with human dignity and with the welfare of the family and of society, prevents their participation, on equal terms with men, in the political, social, economic and cultural life of their countries and is an obstacle to the full development of the potentialities of women in the service of their countries and of humanity,

Bearing in mind the great contribution made by women in social, political, economic and cultural life and the part they play in the family and particularly in the rearing of children,

Convinced that the full and complete development of a country, the welfare of the world and the cause of peace require the maximum participation of women as well as men in all fields,

Considering that it is necessary to ensure the universal recognition in law and in fact of the principle of equality of men and women,

Solemnly proclaims this Declaration:

Article 1

Discrimination against women, denying or limiting as it does their equality of rights with men, is fundamentally unjust and constitutes an offence against human dignity.

Article 2

All appropriate measures shall be taken to abolish existing laws, customs, regulations and practices which are discriminatory against women, and to establish adequate legal protection for equal rights of men and women, in particular:

(a) The principle of equality of rights shall be embodied in the constitution or otherwise guaranteed by law;

(b) The international instruments of the United Nations and the specialized agencies relating to the elimination of discrimination against women shall be ratified or acceded to and fully implemented as soon as practicable.

Article 3

All appropriate measures shall be taken to educate public opinion and to direct national aspirations towards the eradication of prejudice and the abolition of customary and all other practices which are based on the idea of the inferiority of women.

Article 4

All appropriate measures shall be taken to ensure to women on equal terms with men, without any discrimination:

(a) The right to vote in all elections and be eligible for election to all publicly elected bodies;

(b) The right to vote in all public referenda;

(c) The right to hold public office and to exercise all public functions.

Such rights shall be guaranteed by legislation.

Article 5

Women shall have the same rights as men to acquire, change or retain their nationality. Marriage to an alien shall not automatically affect the nationality of the wife either by rendering her stateless or by forcing upon her the nationality of her husband.

Article 6

1. Without prejudice to the safeguarding of the unity and the harmony of the family, which remains the basic unit of any society, all appropriate measures, particularly legilative measures, shall be taken to ensure to women, married or unmarried, equal rights with men in the field of civil law, and in particular:

(a) The right to acquire, administer, enjoy, dispose of and inherit property, including property acquired during marriage;

(b) The right to equality in legal capacity and the exercise thereof;

(c) The same rights as men with regard to the law on the movement of persons.

2. All appropriate measures shall be taken to ensure the principle of equality of status of the husband and wife, and in particular:

(a) Women shall have the same right as men to free choice of a spouse and to enter into marriage only with their free and full consent;

(b) Women shall have equal rights with men during marriage and at its dissolution. In all cases the interest of the children shall be paramount;

(c) Parents shall have equal rights and duties
in matters relating to their children. In
all cases the interest of the children shall
be paramount.

3. Child marriage and the betrothal of young girls
before puberty shall be prohibited, and effective action,
including legislation, shall be taken to specify a
minimum age for marriage and to make the registration of
marriages in an official registry compulsory.

Article 7

All provisions of penal codes which constitute
discrimination against women shall be repealed.

Article 8

All appropriate measures, including legislation,
shall be taken to combat all forms of traffic in women
and exploitation of prostitution of women.

Article 9

All appropriate measures shall be taken to ensure to
girls and women, married or unmarried, equal rights with
men in education at all levels, and in particular:

(a) Equal conditions of access to, and study in,
educational institutions of all types,
including universities and vocational,
technical and professional schools;

(b) The same choice of curricula, the same
examinations, teaching staff with
qualifications of the same standards, and
school premises and equipment of the same
quality, whether the institutions are
co-educational or not;

(c) Equal opportunities to benefit from
scholarships and other study grants;

(d) Equal opportunities for access to programmes of continuing education, including adult literacy programmes;

(e) Access to educational information to help in ensuring the health and well-being of families.

Article 10

1. All appropriate measures shall be taken to ensure to women, married or unmarried, equal rights with men in the field of economic and social life, and in particular:

(a) The right, without discrimination on grounds of marital status or any other grounds, to receive vocational training, to work, to free choice of profession and employment, and to professional and vocational advancement;

(b) The right to equal remuneration with men and to equality of treatment in respect of work of equal value;

(c) The right to leave with pay, retirement privileges and provision for security in respect of unemployment, sickness, old age or other incapacity to work;

(d) The right to receive family allowances on equal terms with men.

2. In order to prevent discrimination against women on account of marriage or maternity and to ensure their effective right to work, measures shall be taken to prevent their dismissal in the event of marriage or maternity and to provide paid maternity leave, with the guarantee of returning to former employment, and to provide the necessary social services, including childcare facilities.

3. Measures taken to protect women in certain types of work, for reasons inherent in their physical nature, shall not be regarded as discriminatory.

Article 11

1. The principle of equality of rights of men and women demands implementation in all States in accordance with the principles of the Charter of the United Nations and of the Universal Declaration of Human Rights.

2. Governments, nongovernmental organizations and individuals are urged, therefore, to do all in their power to promote the implementation of the principles contained in this Declaration.

20. Declaration of Mexico on the Equality of Women and Their Contribution to Development and Peace

Background

The Declaration of Mexico was adopted by the World Conference of the International Women's Year, the first major international conference devoted to women's concerns. The conference was held in Mexico City from June 19 to July 2, 1975. There were 133 countries represented, 10 intergovernmental groups, 23 United Nations specialized agencies, 8 liberation movements, and 113 nongovernmental organizations.

The Declaration of Mexico draws a connection between women's status and the general political and economic international system. It emphasizes the need for implementing the New International Economic Order and also refers to a need for international cooperation to eliminate colonialism, foreign occupation, apartheid, and zionism. The latter reference was a source of serious controversy; it, rather than the provisions on improving the status of women, directly accounts for the negative votes and abstentions. The Declaration was adopted 89 to 3 with 18 abstentions.[1]

Text

The World Conference of the International Women's Year,

Aware that the problems of women, who constitute half of the world's population, are the problems of society as a whole, and that changes in the present ecomomic, political and social situation of women must become an integral part of efforts to transform the

----

[1] The countries which voted against the Declaration were: Denmark, Israel, and the United States.

structures and attitudes that hinder the genuine
satisfaction of their needs,

Recognizing that international co-operation based on
the principles of the Charter of the United Nations
should be developed and strengthened in order to find
solutions to world problems and to build an international
community based on equity and justice,

Recalling that in subscribing to the Charter, the
peoples of the United Nations undertook specific
commitments: "to save succeeding generations from the
scourge of war ..., to reaffirm faith in fundamental
human rights, in the dignity and worth of the human
person, in the equal rights of men and women and of
nations large and small, and to promote social progress
and better standards of life in larger freedom",

Taking note of the fact that since the creation of
the United Nations very important instruments have been
adopted, among which the following constitute landmarks:
the Universal Declaration of Human Rights, the
Declaration on the Granting of Independence to Colonial
Countries and Peoples, the International Development
Strategy for the Second United Nations Development
Decade, and the Declaration and Programme of Action for
the Establishment of a New International Economic Order
based on the Charter of Economic Rights and Duties of
States,

Taking into account that the United Nations
Declaration on the Elimination of Discrimination against
Women considers that: "discrimination against women is
incompatible with human dignity and with the welfare of
the family and of society, prevents their participation,
on equal terms with men, in the political, social,
economic and cultural life of their countries and is an
obstacle to the full development of the potentialities of
women in the service of their countries and of humanity",

Recalling that the General Assembly, in its
resolution 3010 (XXVII) of 18 December 1972, proclaimed
1975 as International Women's Year and that the Year was
to be devoted to intensified action with a view to:
promoting equality between men and women, ensuring the
integration of women in the total development effort, and
increasing the contribution of women to the strengthening
of world peace,

Recalling further that the Economic and Social
Council, in its resolution 1849 (LVI) of 16 May 1974,
adopted the Programme for International Women's Year, and

that the General Assembly, in its resolution 3275 (XXIX) of 10 December 1974, called for full implementation of the Programme,

Taking into account the role played by women in the history of humanity, especially in the struggle for national liberation, the strengthening of international peace, and the elimination of imperialism, colonialism, neo-colonialism, foreign occupation, zionism, alien domination, racism and apartheid,

Stressing that greater and equal participation of women at all levels of decision-making shall decisively contribute to accelerating the pace of development and the maintenance of peace,

Stressing also that women and men of all countries should have equal rights and duties and that it is the task of all States to create the necessary conditions for the attainment and the exercise thereof,

Recognizing that women of the entire world, whatever differences exist between them, share the painful experience of receiving or having received unequal treatment, and that as their awareness of this phenomenon increases they will become natural allies in the struggle against any form of oppression, such as is practised under colonialism, neo-colonialism, zionism, racial discrimination and apartheid thereby constituting an enormous revolutionay potential for economic and social change in the world today,

Recognizing that changes in the social and economic structure of societies, even though they are among the prerequisites, cannot of themselves ensure an immediate improvement in the status of a group which has long been disadvantaged, and that urgent consideration must therefore be given to the full, immediate and early integration of women into national and international life,

Emphasizing that under-development imposes upon women a double burden of exploitation, which must be rapidly eliminated, and that full implementation of national development policies designed to fulfil this objective is seriously hindered by the existing inequitable system of international economic relations,

Aware that the role of women in child-bearing should not be the cause of inequality and discrimination, and that child-rearing demands shared responsibilities among women, men and society as a whole,

Recognizing also the urgency of improving the status of women and finding more effective methods and strategies which will enable them to have the same opportunities as men to participate actively in the development of their countries and to contribute to the attainment of world peace,

Convinced that women must play an important role in the promotion, achievement and maintenance of international peace, and that it is necessay to encourage their efforts towards peace, through their full participation in the national and international organizations that exist for this purpose,

Considering that it is necessary to promote national, regional and international action, in which the implementation of the World Plan of Action adopted by the World Conference of the International Women's Year should make a significant contribution, for the attainment of equality, development and peace,

Decides to promulgate the following principles:

1. Equality between women and men means equality in their dignity and worth as human beings as well as equality in their rights, opportunities and responsibilities.

2. All obstacles that stand in the way of enjoyment by women of equal status with men must be eliminated in order to ensure their full integration into national development and their participation in securing and in maintaining international peace.

3. It is the responsibility of the State to create the necessary facilities so that women may be integrated into society while their children receive adequate care.

4. National nongovernmental organizations should contribute to the advancement of women by assisting women to take advantage of their opportunities, by promoting education and information about women's rights, and by co-operating with their respective Governments.

5. Women and men have equal rights and responsibilities in the family and in society. Equality between women and men should be guaranteed in the family, which is the basic unit of society and where human relations are nurtured. Men should participate more actively, creatively and responsibly in family life for its sound development in order to enable women to be more intensively involved in the activities of their

communities and with a view to combining effectively home and work possibilities of both partners.

6. Women, like men, require opportunities for developing their intellectual potential to the maximum. National policies and programmes should therefore provide them with full and equal access to education and training at all levels, while ensuring that such programmes and policies consciously orient them towards new occupations and new roles consistent with their need for self-fulfilment and the needs of national development.

7. The right of women to work, to receive equal pay for work of equal value, to be provided with equal conditions and opportunities for advancement in work, and all other women's rights to full and satisfying economic activity are strongly reaffirmed. Review of these principles for their effective implementation is now urgently needed, considering the necessity of restructuring world economic relationships. This restructuring offers greater possibilities for women to be integrated into the stream of national economic, social, political and cultural life.

8. All means of communication and information as well as all cultural media should regard as a high priority their responsibility for helping to remove the attitudinal and cultural factors that still inhibit the development of women and for projecting in positive terms the value to society of the assumption by women of changing and expanding roles.

9. Necessary resources should be made available in order that women may be able to participate in the political life of their countries and of the international community since their active participation in national and world affairs at decision-making and other levels in the political field is a prerequisite of women's full exercise of equal rights as well as of their further development and of the national well-being.

10. Equality of rights carries with it corresponding responsibilities; it is therefore a duty of women to make full use of opportunities available to them and to perform their duties to the family, the country and humanity.

11. It should be one of the principal aims of social education to teach respect for physical integrity and its rightful place in human life. The human body, whether that of woman or man, is inviolable and respect for it is a fundamental element of human dignity and freedom.

12. Every couple and every individual has the right to decide freely and responsibly whether or not to have children as well as to determine their number and spacing, and to have information, education and means to do so.

13. Respect for human dignity encompasses the right of every woman to decide freely for herself whether or not to contract matrimony.

14. The issue of inequality, as it affects the vast majority of the women of the world, is closely linked with the problem of under-development, which exists as a result not only of unsuitable internal structures but also of a profoundly unjust world economic system.

15. The full and complete development of any country requires the maximum participation of women as well as of men in all fields; the under-utilization of the potential of approximately half of the world's population is a serious obstacle to social and economic development.

16. The ultimate end of development is to achieve a better quality of life for all, which means not only the development of economic and other material resources but also the physical, moral, intellectual and cultural growth of the human person.

17. In order to integrate women into development, States should undertake the necessary changes in their economic and social policies because women have the right to participate and contribute to the total development effort.

18. The present state of international economic relations poses serious obstacles to a more efficient utilization of all human and material potential for accelerated development and for the improvement of living standards in developing countries aimed at the elimination of hunger, child mortality, unemployment, illiteracy, ignorance and backwardness, which concern all of humanity and women in particular. It is therefore essential to establish and implement with urgency the New International Economic Order, of which the Charter of Economic Rights and Duties of States constitutes a basic element, founded on equity, sovereign equality, interdependence, common interest, co-operation among all States irrespective of their social and economic systems, on the principles of peaceful coexistence and on the promotion by the entire international community of economic and social progress of all countries, especially

developing countries, and on the progress of States comprising the international community.

19. The principle of the full and permanent sovereignty of every State over its natural resources, wealth and all economic activities, and its inalienable right of nationalization as an expression of this sovereignty constitute fundamental prerequisites in the process of economic and social development.

20. The attainment of economic and social goals, so basic to the realization of the rights of women, does not, however, of itself bring about the full integration of women in development on a basis of equality with men unless specific measures are undertaken for the elimination of all forms of discrimination against them. It is therefore important to formulate and implement models of development that will promote the participation and advancement of women in all fields of work and provide them with equal educational opportunities and such services as would facilitate housework.

21. Modernization of the agricultural sector of vast areas of the world is an indispensable element for progress, particularly as it creates opportunities for millions of rural women to participate in development. Governments, the United Nations, its specialized agencies and other competent regional and international organizations should support projects designed to utilize the maximum potential and develop the self-reliance of rural women.

22. It must be emphasized that, given the required economic, social and legal conditions as well as the appropriate attitudes conducive to the full and equal participation of women in society, efforts and measures aimed at a more intensified integration of women in development can be successfully implemented only if made an integral part of over-all social and economic growth. Full participation of women in the various economic, social, political and cultural sectors is an important indication of the dynamic progress of peoples and their development. Individual human rights can be realized only within the framework of total development.

23. The objectives considered in this Declaration can be achieved only in a world in which the relations between States are governed, inter alia, by the following principles: the sovereign equality of States, the free self-determination of peoples, the unacceptability of acquisition or attempted acquisition of territories by force and the prohibition of recognition of such acquisition, territorial integrity, and the right to

defend it, and non-interference in the domestic affairs of States, in the same manner as relations between human beings should be governed by the supreme principle of the equality of rights of women and men.

24. International co-operation and peace require the achievement of national liberation and independence, the elimination of colonialism and neo-colonialism, foreign occupation, zionism, apartheid, and racial discrimination in all its forms as well as the recognition of the dignity of peoples and their right to self-determination.

25. Women have a vital role to play in the promotion of peace in all spheres of life: in the family, the community, the nation and the world. Women must participate equally with men in the decision-making processes which help to promote peace at all levels.

26. Women and men together should eliminate colonialism, neo-colonialism, imperialism, foreign domination and occupation, zionism, apartheid, racial discrimination, the acquisition of land by force and the recognition of such acquisition, since such practices inflict incalculable suffering on women, men and children.

27. The solidarity of women in all countries of the world should be supported in their protest against violations of human rights condemned by the United Nations. All forms of repression and inhuman treatment of women, men and children, including imprisonment, torture, massacres, collective punishment, destruction of homes, forced eviction and arbitrary restriction of movement shall be considered crimes against humanity and in violation of the Universal Declaration of Human Rights and other international instruments.

28. Women all over the world should unite to eliminate violations of human rights committed against women and girls such as: rape, prostitution, physical assault, mental cruelty, child marriage, forced marriage and marriage as a commercial transaction.

29. Peace requires that women as well as men should reject any type of intervention in the domestic affairs of States, whether it be openly or covertly carried on by other States or by transnational corporations. Peace also requires that women as well as men should also promote respect for the sovereign right of a State to establish its own economic, social and political system without undergoing political and economic pressures or coercion of any type.

30. Women as well as men should promote real, general and complete disarmament under effective international control, starting with nuclear disarmament. Until genuine disarmament is achieved, women and men throughout the world must maintain their vigilance and do their utmost to achieve and maintain international peace.

Wherefore,

The World Conference of the International Women's Year

1. Affirms its faith in the objectives of the International Women's Year, which are equality, development and peace;

2. Proclaims its commitment to the achievement of such objectives;

3. Strongly urges Governments, the entire United Nations system, regional and international intergovernmental organizations and the international community as a whole to dedicate themselves to the creation of a just society where women, men and children can live in dignity, freedom, justice and prosperity.

21. The World Plan of Action for the Implementation of the Objectives of the International Women's Year

Background

International Women's Year was proclaimed by the General Assembly in Resolution 3010 (XXVII) of December 18, 1972. The World Plan was adopted by the World Conference of the International Women's Year which was held in Mexico City in 1975 (see p.201 above). The objective of the World Plan is to ensure equality of women with men and to advance the status of women at national and international levels. The plan addresses a wide range of issues and outlines strategies for improving the treatment of women in administrative, political, legislative, employment, education and other areas. It particularly emphasizes the need to redefine sex roles within the family and aims at eliminating sexual discrimination in all its forms. It was adopted without a vote. It is not a treaty and, therefore, is not legally binding.

Summary

The Plan consists of five major sections, an introduction, and a concluding review. The introduction sets forth the basic principles of equality of men and women and the objective of eliminating discrimination based on sex. It cites the major documents and United Nations resolutions and it refers to the special needs of Third World women. It also stresses the desirability of redefining sex roles, increasing male participation in domestic areas and providing services to facilitate female participation in the economic, social, and poltical lives of their countries.

Section I, National Action, includes guidelines for national action calling for research, commissions, action groups, and coordination with other levels of governmental activity in order to bring about the goals of the Plan. It also emphasizes the importance of nongovernmental women's organizations in achieving these objectives. The Plan calls for constitutional and legislative measures guaranteeing equality between the sexes and for participation of women in all stages of the planning and implementation of the programs established under the Plan. The Plan states the belief that women may not be aware of their rights, and that States must provide special measures to alert women to their opportunities and provide education to make it possible for them to maximize their potential. Some of the minimal achievements the Plan suggests are: increased literacy among females; extension of technical educational programs to women; reduction of unemployment among women; enactment of legislation increasing women's political rights; increased provision of health care to women; recognition of the economic value of women's work in the domestic sphere, food production, and voluntary services; and reevaluation of formal and informal educational systems with a view to altering sex role stereotyping.

Section II, Specific Areas for National Action, develops strategies for governmental and nongovernmental work. There are nine areas which are highlighted. The first is "International cooperation and the strengthening of international peace." Here the issues of human rights and the building of friendly relations between states are discussed, relating them to the special needs of women. International organizations are called upon to involve women in their preparation and action on these topics and are encouraged to design educational, cultural, scientific, and other internaional exchange programs to facilitate transnational communication and understanding.

The second is "Political Participation" which points out the discrepancy between women's numbers in the population and their representation in political decision-making groups. Special measures are advised for changing legal requirements and for actively recruiting women into all levels of political action. In addition special campaigns are called for to enlighten the public to the particular contributions of women and to draw females of all ages into rural, community, and urban leadership training and development programs.

The third area, "Education and Training," begins with the point that in most States, women's literacy and women's enrollment in education and training programs is substantially below that of men's. There is a call for educational programs for all ages combined with inexpensive child-care to enable women to attend classes. The Plan urges the establishment of target dates for the elimination of illiteracy and special programs, especially in rural areas, to make the objectives realizable. In addition it suggests that textbooks and other materials should be reevaluated to ensure that they reflect a positive image of women in society; it also encourages cooeducation. The mass media is called upon to inform women and and girls of their opportunities and rights and to take all possible steps to bring about a change in community attitudes towards women.

The fourth topic, "Employment and Related Economic Roles," provides information about the major contribution of women to the economy and the absence of comparable pay or recognition for this work, as well as the limited opportunities for women to advance economically. There is a call for legislative and administrative programs to eliminate discrimination in the economic domain, and to encourage the establishment of cooperatives and small scale industries. Special targets are called for setting substantial increases of females in skilled and technical work and special efforts to increase their numbers in industrial and commercial management positions. Governments, private employers, and trade unions should guarantee women the right to maternity leave which does not affect their employment status.

The fifth area addressed is "Health and Nutrition." Special emphasis is laid upon adequate food and health care as necessary to the fulfillment of the individual's potential in all spheres. Governments are called upon to establish health care programs and to make health care available in rural areas, particularly to pregnant and nursing women and to all children regardless of sex. Since women are important providers of health care, they are to be included in training and health care programs at all levels. Also, programs are called for to inform women about nutrition to enable them to take better care of themselves and their families and communities are urged to make sanitary preservation of food a major priority at the local level.

The sixth topic, "The Family in Modern Society," points out the need for free consent to marriage, minimum age for marriage, and public registation of marriages. A call is made to provide women when married with equal rights to property, to work, to decisions regarding children, and to equal status at the dissolution of a marriage. Special attention is paid to the needs of unmarried women and to single parent families. A call is made for recognition of the special contribution and importance of each family member and the desirability of raising the status of all domestic roles performed by men and women in the home.

The seventh area is "Population" and stresses the link between the status of women and family size. Women are entitled to adequate information and means to freely determine the number and spacing of their children.

States are also called upon to consider the effect of migration, urbanization, and rural development on family life and on the working lives of women. The Plan also suggests that decentralization of education and health facilities could have a positive impact on rural life.

The eighth topic which is covered is "Housing and Related Facilities." Here the Plan considers the heavier influence on women than men of the conditions of housing and neighborhoods since women are more likely to spend a greater part of the time in and around the home. States are called upon to involve women in the planning and design of housing and neighborhoods and to pay special attention to accessibility for women and children of vital needs and to neighborhood centers.

The final topic discussed is "Other Social Questions." Governments are encouraged to develop social services, including women in the process, and making use of nongovernmental organizations as much as possible. The needs of women among migrant workers, slum dwellers, the elderly, and the indigent are addressed. Attention is also paid to female criminality and female offenders and States are encouraged to ratify the relevant treaties and take steps to eliminate traffic in persons and rehabilitate the victims of trade in women and young girls.

The third section of the World Plan of Action is entitled "Research, Data Collection and Analysis." It discusses the need for accurate information in order to define and design solutions to problems obstructing the advancement of women. The necessity of data collection at all levels is stressed and several special needs are defined which include: participation of women in national planning and policy-making; the extent of women's activities in food production, water and fuel supply, and other basic services for which they are not now reimbursed; the economic and social contribution of housework and home-based economic activities; the relative time spent on household activities and on leisure by girls and women relative to boys and men; and the quality of life. The United Nations is called upon to use their resources to aid in the collection of data and dissemination of resulting reports.

A special section of the Plan is devoted to "Mass Media." This portion of the Plan begins by observing that public attitudes and values constitute a major obstacle to the improvement of women's status in society. Rather than reinforcing these attitudes, as it does at present, the media is identified as a great potential for altering negative images of the roles and potential of women. The media is defined as including public channels of communication such as radio, television, and press, but also traditional forms of entertainment in the oral altering negative images of the roles and potential of women. The media is defined as including public channels of communication such as radio, television, and press, but also traditional forms of entertainment in the oral and dramatic mode which are common in rural areas. Governments are called upon to support research at national, regional, and international levels to determine the effects of the media on the public and to take steps to ensure that the information and programming raises' public consciousness about changing sex roles and the need to project a more dynamic image of women. Those responsible should inform the public about historical and contemporary contributions of women and appoint women to a variety of positions in the media including management.

The fifth section "International and Regional Action" is divided into a global section which urges the establishment of a United Nations decade for women and a regional section which emphasizes the role of the existing United Nations regional commissions. The global section points out the need to increase women in policy and planning at the international level, including positions at the United Nations. It then outlines programatic activities for 1)technical cooperation, 2)formulation and implementation of international standards, and 3) exchange of information and experience. The regional section indicates how the existing commisions can foster the effectiveness of all three sets of activities.

The final section of the Plan, "Review and Appraisal," calls for periodic and regular meetings to assess and evaluate action to implement the Plan. These reviews are urged at all levels of action, national, regional and global. Organizations at all three levels are encouraged to coordinate their activities and to make use of existing programs and agencies when possible. Governments are asked to consider the World Plan when they formulate their development programs and to consider its implementation a national priority by allocating appropriate and sufficient financial and administrative support.

For a text of the World Plan of Action in its entirety see: United Nations, Report of the World Conference of the International Women's Year (New York: United Nations, 1976). pp. 8-41. United Nations document number E/Conf.66/34.

22. Convention on the Elimination of All Forms of Discrimination Against Women

Background

The Convention was drafted by the Commission on the Status of Women as a comprehensive legally binding treaty to codify the principles of the Declaration on the Elimination of Discrimination Against Women and other norms as well. The work on this treaty began in 1974, was officially authorized by the General Assembly in Resolution 3521 (XXX) on December 15, 1975, and was completed and adopted by the Commission on December 17, 1976. After consideration by the Third Committee (Social, Cultural and Humanitarian) and the Economic and Social Council, it was transmitted to and adopted by the General Assembly in Resolution 34/180 on December 18, 1979, by a vote of 130-0 with 10 abstentions. The treaty came into force on September 3, 1981, in accordance with Article 27, thirty days after the deposit of the twentieth instrument of ratification.

The Convention reiterates the norm of non-discrimination on the basis of sex and reaffirms the goal of equality between men and women. It covers a full range of subjects, including many which were the basis for earlier more specific instruments, such as those on slave trade, traffic in women, nationality, education, and employment. It also covers some new topics, in particular, the special problems of rural women. It includes obligations of States to foster acceptance of joint parental responsibilities within the family and efforts to eliminate sex-role stereotyping.

Text

Preamble

The States Parties to the present Convention,

Noting that the Charter of the United Nations reaffirms faith in fundamental human rights, in the dignity and worth of the human person and in the equal rights of men and women,

Noting that the Universal Declaration of Human Rights affirms the principle of the inadmissibility of discrimination and proclaims that all human beings are born free and equal in dignity and rights and that everyone is entitled to all the rights and freedoms set forth therein, without distinction of any kind, including distinction based on sex,

Noting that the States Parties to the International Covenants on Human Rights have the obligation to ensure the equal right of men and women to enjoy all economic, social, cultural, civil and political rights,

Considering the international conventions concluded under the auspices of the United Nations and the specialized agencies promoting equality of rights of men and women,

Noting also the resolutions, declarations and recommendations adopted by the United Nations and the specialized agencies promoting equality of rights of men and women,

Concerned, however, that despite these various instruments extensive discrimination against women continues to exist,

Recalling that discrimination against women violates the principles of equality of rights and respect for human dignity, is an obstacle to the participation of women, on equal terms with men, in the political, social, economic and cultural life of their countries, hampers the growth of the prosperity of society and the family and makes more difficult the full development of the potentialities of women in the service of their countries and of humanity,

Concerned that in situations of poverty women have the least access to food, health, education, training and opportunities for employment and other needs,

Convinced that the establishment of the new international economic order based on equity and justice will contribute significantly towards the promotion of equality between men and women,

Emphasizing that the eradication of apartheid, of all forms of racism, racial discrimination, colonialism, neo-colonialism, aggression, foreign occupation and domination and interference in the internal affairs of States is essential to the full enjoyment of the rights of men and women,

Affirming that the strengthening of international peace and security, relaxation of international tension, mutual co-operation among all States irrespective of their social and economic systems, general and complete disarmament, and in particular nuclear disarmament under strict and effective international control, the affirmation of the principles of justice, equality and mutual benefit in relations among countries and the realization of the right of peoples under alien and colonial domination and foreign occupation to self-determination and independence, as well as respect for national sovereignty and territorial integrity, will promote social progress and development and as a consequence will contribute to the attainment of full equality between men and women,

Convinced that the full and complete development of a country, the welfare of the world and the cause of peace require the maximum participation of women on equal terms with men in all fields,

Bearing in mind the great contribution of women to the welfare of the family and to the development of society, so far not fully recognized, the social significance of maternity and the role of both parents in the family and in the upbringing of children, and aware that the role of women in procreation should not be a basis for discrimination but that the upbringing of children requires a sharing of responsibility between men and women and society as a whole,

Aware that a change in the traditional role of men as well as the role of women in society and in the family is needed to achieve full equality between men and women,

Determined to implement the principles set forth in the Declaration on the Elimination of Discrimination against Women and, for that purpose, to adopt the measures required for the elimination of such discrimination in all its forms and manifestations,

Have agreed on the following:

PART I

Article 1

For the purposes of the present Convention, the term
"discrimination against women" shall mean any distiction,
exclusion or restriction made on the basis of sex which
has the effect or purpose of impairing or nullifying the
recognition, enjoyment or exercise by women, irrespective
of their marital status, on a basis of equality of men
and women, of human rights and fundamental freedoms in
the poitical, economic, social, cultural, civil or any
other field.

Article 2

States Parties condemn discrimination against women
in all its forms, agree to pursue by all appropriate
means and without delay a policy of eliminating
discrimination against women and, to this end, undertake:

(a) To embody the principle of the equality of
    men and women in their national
    constitutions or other appropriate
    legislation if not yet incorporated therein
    and to ensure, through law and other
    appropriate means, the practical realization
    of this principle;

(b) To adopt appropriate legislative and other
    measures, including sanctions where
    appropriate, prohibiting all discrimination
    against women;

(c) To establish legal protection of the rights
    of women on an equal basis with men and to
    ensure through competent national tribunals
    and other public institutions the effective
    protection of women against any act of
    discrimination;

(d) To refrain from engaging in any act or practice of discrimination against women and to ensure that public authorities and institutions shall act in conformity with this obligation;

(e) To take all appropriate measures to eliminate discrimination against women by any person, organization or enterprise;

(f) To take all appropriate measures, including legislation, to modify or abolish existing laws, regulations, customs and practices which constitute discrimination against women;

(g) To repeal all national penal provisions which constitute discrimination against women.

Article 3

States Parties shall take in all fields, in particular in the political, social, economic and cultural fields, all appropriate measures, including legislation, to ensure the full development and advancement of women, for the purpose of guaranteeing them the exercise and enjoyment of human rights and fundamental freedoms on a basis of equality with men.

Article 4

1. Adoption by States Parties of temporary special measures aimed at accelerating de facto equality between men and women shall not be considered discrimination as defined in the present convention, but shall in no way entail as a consequence the maintenance of unequal or separate standards; these measures shall be discontinued when the objectives of equality of opportunity and treatment have been achieved.

2. Adoption by States Parties of special measures, including those measures contained in the present Convention, aimed at protecting maternity shall not be considered discriminatory.

Article 5

States Parties shall take all appropriate measures:

(a) To modify the social and cultural patterns of conduct of men and women, with a view to achieving the elimination of prejudices and customary and all other practices which are based on the idea of the inferiority or the superiority of either of the sexes or on stereotyped roles for men and women;

(b) To ensure that family education includes a proper understanding of maternity as a social function and the recognition of the common responsibility of men and women in the upbringing and development of their children, it being understood that the interest of the children is the primordial consideration in all cases.

Article 6

States Parties shall take all appropriate measures, including legislation, to suppress all forms of traffic in women and exploitation of prostitution of women.

PART II

Article 7

States Parties shall take all appropriate measures to eliminate discrimination against women in the political and public life of the country and, in particular, shall ensure to women, on equal terms with men, the right:

(a) To vote in all elections and public referenda and to be eligible for election to all publicly elected bodies;

(b) To participate in the formulation of government policy and the implementation

thereof and to hold public office and
perform all public functions at all levels
of government;

(c) To participate in nongovernmental
organizations and associations concerned
with the public and political life of the
country.

Article 8

States Parties shall take all appropriate measures
to ensure to women, on equal terms with men and without
any discrimination, the opportunity to represent their
Governments at the international level and to participate
in the work of international organizations.

Article 9

1. States Parties shall grant women equal rights
with men to acquire, change or retain their nationality.
They shall ensure in particular that neither marriage to
an alien nor change of nationality by the husband during
marriage shall automatically change the nationality of
the wife, render her stateless or force upon her the
nationality of the husband.

2. States Parties shall grant women equal rights
with men with respect to the nationality of their
children.

Part III

Article 10

States Parties shall take all appropriate measures
to eliminate discrimination against women in order to
ensure to them equal rights with men in the field of
education and in particular to ensure, on a basis of
equality of men and women:

(a) The same conditions for career and vocational guidance, for access to studies and for the achievement of diplomas in educational establishments of all categories in rural as well as in urban areas; this equality shall be ensured in pre-school, general, technical, professional and higher technical education, as well as in all types of vocational training;

(b) Access to the same curricula, the same examinations, teaching staff with qualifications of the same standard and school premises and equipment of the same quality;

(c) The elimination of any stereotyped concept of the roles of men and women at all levels and in all forms of education by encouraging coeducation and other types of education which will help to achieve this aim and, in particular, by the revision of textbooks and school programmes and the adaptation of teaching methods;

(d) The same opportunities to benefit from scholarships and other study grants;

(e) The same opportunities for access to programmes of continuing education, including adult and functional literacy programmes, particularly those aimed at reducing, at the earliest possible time, any gap in education existing between men and women;

(f) The reduction of female student drop-out rates and the organization of programmes for girls and women who have left school prematurely;

(g) The same opportunities to participate actively in sports and physical education;

(h) Access to specific educational information to help to ensure the health and well-being of families, including information and advice on family planning.

Article 11

1. States Parties shall take all appropriate measures to eliminate discrimination against women in the field of employment in order to ensure, on a basis of equality of men and women, the same rights, in particular:

(a) The right to work as an inalienable right of all human beings;

(b) The right to the same employment opportunities, including the application of the same criteria for selection in matters of employment;

(c) The right to free choice of profession and employment, the right to promotion, job security and all benefits and conditions of service and the right to receive vocational training and retraining, including apprenticeships, advanced vocational training and recurrent training;

(d) The right to equal remuneration, including benefits, and to equal treatment in respect of work of equal value, as well as equality of treatment in the evaluation of the quality of work;

(e) The right to social security, particularly in cases of retirement, unemployment, sickness, invalidity and old age and other incapacity to work, as well as the right to paid leave;

(f) The right to protection of health and to safety in working conditions, including the safeguarding of the function of reproduction.

2. In order to prevent discrimination against women on the grounds of marriage or maternity and to ensure their effective right to work, States Parties shall take appropriate measures:

(a) To prohibit, subject to the imposition of sanctions, dismissal on the grounds of pregnancy or of maternity leave and discrimination in dismissals on the basis of marital status;

(b) To introduce maternity leave with pay or with comparable social benefits without loss of former employment, seniority or social allowances;

(c) To encourage the provision of the necessary supporting social services to enable parents to combine family obligations with work responsibilities and participation in public life, in particular through promoting the establishment and development of a network of child-care facilities;

(d) To provide special protection to women during pregnancy in types of work proved to be harmful to them.

3. Protective legislation relating to matters covered in this article shall be reviewed periodically in the light of scientific and technological knowledge and shall be revised, repealed or extended as necessary.

Article 12

1. States Parties shall take all appropriate measures to eliminate discrimination against women in he field of health care in order to ensure, on a basis of equality of men and women, access to health care services, including those related to family planning.

2. Notwithstanding the provisions of paragraph 1 of this article, States Parties shall ensure to women appropriate services in connexion with pregnancy, confinement and the post-natal period, granting free services where necessary, as well as adequate nutrition during pregnancy and lactation.

Article 13

States Parties shall take all appropriate measures to eliminate discrimination against women in other areas of economic and social life in order to ensure, on a basis of equality of men and women, the same rights, in particular:

(a) The right to family benefits;

(b) The right to bank loans, mortgages and other forms of financial credit;

(c) The right to participate in recreational activities, sports and all aspects of cultural life.

Article 14

1. States Parties shall take into account the particular problems faced by rural women and the significant roles which rural women play in the economic survival of their families, including their work in the non-monetized sectors of the economy, and shall take all appropriate measures to ensure the application of the provisions of this Convention to women in rural areas.

2. States Parties shall take all appropriate measures to eliminate discrimination against women in rural areas in order to ensure, on a basis of equality of men and women, that they participate in and benefit from rural development and, in particular, shall ensure to such women the right:

(a) To participate in the elaboration and implementation of development planning at all levels;

(b) To have access to adequate health care facilities, including information, counselling and services in family planning;

(c) To benefit directly from social security programmes;

(d) To obtain all types of training and education, formal and non-formal, including that relating to functional literacy, as well as, inter alia, the benefit of all community and extension services, in order to increase their technical proficiency;

(e) To organize self-help groups and co-operatives in order to obtain equal access to economic opportunities through employment or self-employment;

(f) To participate in all community activities;

(g) To have access to agricultural credit and loans, marketing facilities, appropriate technology and equal treatment in land and agrarian reform as well as in land resettlement schemes;

(h) To enjoy adequate living conditions, particularly in relation to housing, sanitation, electricity and water supply, transport and communications.

PART IV

Article 15

1. States Parties shall accord to women equality with men before the law.

2. States Parties shall accord to women, in civil matters, a legal capacity identical to that of men and the same opportunities to exercise that capacity. In particular, they shall give women equal rights to conclude contracts and to administer property and shall treat them equally in all stages of procedure in courts and tribunals.

3. States Parties agree that all contracts and all other private instruments of any kind with a legal effect which is directed at restricting the legal capacity of women shall be deemed null and void.

4. States Parties shall accord to men and women the same rights with regard to the law relating to the movement of persons and the freedom to choose their residence and domicile.

Article 16

1. States Parties shall take all appropriate measures to eliminate discrimination against women in all matters relating to marriage and family relations and in particular shall ensure, on a basis of equality of men and women:

(a) The same right to enter into marriage;

(b) the same right freely to choose a spouse and to enter into marriage only with their free and full consent;

(c) The same rights and responsibilities during marriage and at its dissolution;

(d) The same rights and responsibilities as parents, irrespective of their marital status, in matters relating to their children; in all cases the interests of the children shall be paramount;

(e) The same rights to decide freely and responsibly on the number and spacing of their children and to have access to the information, education and means to enable them to exercise these rights;

(f) The same rights and responsibilities with regard to guardianship, wardship, trusteeship and adoption of children, or similar institutions where these concepts exist in national legislation; in all cases the interests of the children shall be paramount;

(g) The same personal rights as husband and wife, including the right to choose a family name, a profession and an occupation;

(h) The same rights for both spouses in respect of the ownership, acquisition, management, administration, enjoyment and disposition of property, whether free of charge or for a valuable consideration.

2. The betrothal and the marriage of a child shall have no legal effect, and all necessary action, including legislation, shall be taken to specify a minimum age for marriage and to make the registration of marriages in an official registry compulsory.

PART V

Article 17

1. For the purpose of considering the progress made
in the implementation of the present Convention, there
shall be established a Committee on the Elimination of
Discrimination against Women (hereinafter referred to as
the Committee) consisting, at the time of entry into
force of the Convention, of eighteen and, after
ratification of or accession to the Convention by the
thirty-fifth State Party, of twenty-three experts of high
moral standing and competence in the field covered by the
Convention. The experts shall be elected by States
Parties from among their nationals and shall serve in
their personal capacity, consideration being given to
equitable geographical distribution and to the
representation of the different forms of civilization as
well as the principal legal systems.

2. The members of the Committee shall be elected by
secret ballot from a list of persons nominated by States
Parties. Each State Party may nominate one person from
among its own nationals.

3. The initial election shall be held six months
after the date of the entry into force of the present
Convention. At least three months before the date of
each election the Secretary-General of the United Nations
shall address a letter to the States Parties inviting
them to submit their nominations within two months. The
Secretary-General shall prepare a list in alphabeltical
order of all persons thus nominated, indicating the
States Parties which have nominated them, and shall
submit it to the States Parties.

4. Elections of the members of the Committee shall
be held at a meeting of States Parties convened by the
Secretary-General at United Nations Headquarters. At
that meeting, for which two thirds of the States Parties
shall constitute a quorum, the persons elected to the
Committee shall be those nominees who obtain the largest
number of votes and an absolute majority of the votes of
the representatives of States Parties present and voting.

5. The members of the Committee shall be elected
for a term of four years. However, the terms of nine of
the members elected at the first election shall expire at
the end of two years; immediately after the first

election the names of these nine members shall be chosen by lot by the Chairman of the Committee.

6. The election of the five additional members of the Committee shall be held in accordance with the provisions of paragraphs 2, 3 and 4 of this article, following the thirty-fifth ratification or accession. The terms of two of the additional members elected on this occasion shall expire at the end of two years, the names of these two members having been chosen by lot by the Chairman of the Committee.

7. For the filling of casual vacancies, the State Party whose expert has ceased to function as a member of the Committee shall appoint another expert from among its nationals, subject to the approval of the Committee.

8. The members of the Committee shall, with the approval of the General Assembly, receive emoluments from United Nations resources on such terms and conditions as the Assembly may decide, having regard to the importance of the Committee's responsibilities.

9. The Secretary-General of the United Nations shall provide the necessary staff and facilities for the effective performance of the functions of the Committee under the present Convention.

Article 18

1. States Parties undertake to submit to the Secretary-General of the United Nations, for consideration by the Committee, a report on the legislative, judicial, administrative or other measures which they have adopted to give effect to the provisions of the present Convention and on the progress made in this respect:

(a) Within one year after the entry into force for the State concerned; and

(b) Thereafter at least every four years and further whenever the Committee so requests.

2. Reports may indicate factors and difficulties affecting the degree of fulfilment of obligations under the present Convention.

Article 19

1. The Committee shall adopt its own rules of procedure.

2. The Committee shall elect its officers for a term of two years.

Article 20

1. The Committee shall normally meet for a period of not more than two weeks annually in order to consider the reports submitted in accordance with article 18 of the present Convention.

2. The meetings of the Committee shall normally be held at United Nations Headquarters or at any other convenient place as determined by the Committee.

Article 21

1. The Committee shall, through the Economic and Social Council, report annually to the General Assembly of the United Nations on its activities and may make suggestions and general recommendations based on the examination of reports and information received from the States Parties. Such suggestions and general recommendations shall be included in the report of the Committee together with comments, if any, from States Parties.

2. The Secretary-General shall transmit the reports of the Committee to the Commission on the Status of Women for its information.

Article 22

The specialized agencies shall be entitled to be represented at the consideration of the implementation of such provisions of the present Convention as fall within the scope of their activities. The Committee may invite the specialized agencies to submit reports on the implementation of the Convention in areas falling within the scope of their activities.

PART VI

Article 23

Nothing in this Convention shall affect any provisions that are more conducive to the achievement of equality between men and women which may be contained:

(a) In the legislation of a State Party; or

(b) In any other international convention, treaty or agreement in force for that State.

Article 24

States Parties undertake to adopt all necessary measures at the national level aimed at achieving the full realization of the rights recognized in the present Convention.

Article 25

1. The present Convention shall be open for signature by all States.

2. The Secretary-General of the United Nations is designated as the depositary of the present Convention.

3. The present Convention is subject to ratification. Instruments of ratification shall be deposited with the Secretary-General of the United Nations.

4. The present Convention shall be open to accession by all States. Accession shall be effected by the deposit of an instrument of accession with the Secretary-General of the United Nations.

Article 26

1. A request for the revision of the present Convention may be made at any time by any State Party by means of a notification in writing addressed to the Secretary-General of the United Nations.

2. The General Assembly of the United Nations shall decide upon the steps, if any, to be taken in respect of such a request.

Article 27

1. The present Convention shall enter into force on the thirtieth day after the date of deposit with the Secretary General of the United Nations of the twentieth instrument of ratification or accession.

2. For each State ratifying the present Convention or acceding to it after the deposit of the twentieth instrument of ratification or accession, the Convention shall enter into force on the thirtieth day after the date of the deposit of its own instrument of ratification or accession.

Article 28

1. The Secretary-General of the United Nations shall receive and circulate to all States the text of reservations made by States at the time of ratification or accession.

2. A reservation incompatible with the object and purpose of the present Convention shall not be permitted.

3. Reservations may be withdrawn at any time by notification to this effect addressed to the Secretary-General of the United Nations, who shall then inform all States thereof. Such notification shall take effect on the date on which it is received.

Article 29

1. Any dispute between two or more States Parties concerning the interpretation or application of the present Convention which is not settled by negotiation shall, at the request of one of them, be submitted to arbitration. If within six months from the date of the request for arbitration the parties are unable to agree on the organization of the arbitration, any one of those parties may refer the dispute to the International Court of Justice by request in conformity with the Statute of the Court.

2. Each State Party may at the time of signature or ratification of this Convention or accession thereto declare that it does not consider itself bound by paragraph 1 of this article. The other States Parties shall not be bound by that paragraph with respect to any State Party which has made such a reservation.

3. Any State Party which has made a reservation in accordance with paragraph 2 of this article may at any time withdraw that reservation by notification to the Secretary-General of the United Nations.

Article 30

The present Convention, the Arabic, Chinese, English, French, Russian and Spanish texts of which are equally authentic, shall be deposited with the Secretary-General of the United Nations.

IN WITNESS WHEREOF the undersigned, duly authorized, have signed the present Convention.

Table of Ratifications

Afghanistan+	8/14/80	Burundi+	7/17/80
Argentina+	7/17/80	Byelorussian	
Australia+	7/17/80	SSR*	2/4/81
Austria	3/31/82	Canada*	12/10/81
Barbados	10/16/80	Cape Verde	12/5/80
Belgium+	7/17/80	Chile+*	7/17/80
Benin+	11/11/81	China*	11/4/80
Bhutan	8/31/81	Colombia+	1/19/82
Bolivia+	5/30/80	Congo+	7/29/80
Brazil+*	3/31/81	Costa Rica+	7/17/80
Bulgaria*	2/8/82	Cuba*	7/17/80

Czechoslovakia*	2/16/82	Luxembourg+	7/17/80
Democratic		Madagascar	7/17/80
Kampuchea+	10/17/80	Mexico*	3/23/81
Denmark+	7/17/80	Mongolia*	7/20/81
Dominica	9/15/80	Netherlands+	7/17/80
Dominican		New Zealand+	7/17/80
Republic+	7/17/80	Nicaragua	10/27/81
Ecuador	11/9/81	Norway	5/21/81
Egypt (U. A. R.)*	9/18/81	Panama	10/29/81
El Salvador*	8/19/81	Peru+	7/23/81
Ethiopia*	9/10/81	Philippines	8/5/81
Finland+	7/17/80	Poland*	7/30/80
France+*	7/17/80	Portugal	7/30/80
Gabon+	7/17/80	Romania*	1/7/82
Gambia+	7/29/80	Rwanda	3/2/81
German Democratic		Saint Vincent and	
Republic*	7/9/80	the Grenadines	8/4/81
Germany, Federal		Senegal+	7/29/80
Republic of+	7/17/80	Spain+	7/17/80
Ghana+	7/17/80	Sri Lanka	10/5/81
Grenada+	7/17/80	Sweden	7/2/80
Guatemala+	6/8/80	Tunisia+	7/24/80
Guinea+*	7/17/80	Uganda+	7/30/80
Guinea-Bissau+	7/17/80	Ukrainian SSR*	3/12/81
Guyana	7/17/80	Union of Soviet	
Haiti	7/17/80	Socialist	
Honduras+	6/11/80	Republics*	1/23/81
Hungary*	6/6/80	United Kingdom of	
Iceland+	7/24/80	Great Britain	
India+*	7/30/80	and N.Ireland+*	7/22/81
Indonesia+	7/29/80	United Republic	
Israel+	7/17/80	of Tanzania+	7/17/80
Italy+*	7/17/80	United States of	
Ivory Coast+	7/17/80	America	7/17/80
Jamaica+	7/17/80	Uruguay	10/9/81
Japan+	7/17/80	Venezuela*+	7/17/80
Jordan+*	12/3/80	Viet Nam	2/17/82
Lao People's		Yugoslavia	2/26/82
Democratic		Zaire+	7/17/80
Republic	8/14/81	Zambia+	7/17/80
Lesotho+	7/17/80		

+Indicates signature only.

*Indicates reservation or declaration at time of signature or ratification. Most of the reservations are to the compulsory jurisdiction of the International Court of Justice in connection with dispute settlement (Article 29).

Source: United Nations, Multilateral Treaties Deposited with the Secretary-General: Status as at 31 December 1981 (New York: United Nations, 1982) and United Nations Office of Public Information, UN Monthly Chronicle Vol.XIX (Jan.-July,1982).

23. Programme of Action for the Second Half of the United Nations Decade for Women: Equality, Development and Peace

Background

The Programme of Action was designed for the second half of the United Nations Decade for Women. It was based on an appraisal of the progress made to implement the World Plan of Action during the first half of the decade. The Programme was adopted by the World Conference on Women held in Copenhagen, Denmark, from July 14 to 31, 1980, by a vote of 94 to 4 with 22 abstentions.[1] The Conference was attended by representatives of 145 nation-states as well as observers and participants from international governmental and nongovernmental organizations and other United Nations bodies.

Like the World Plan, the Programme covers a broad range of social, political, economic, and legal issues related to the status of women. It calls for active measures to improve the position of women in all fields, including national and international programs especially designed to advance the status of women. Targets are set for national and international action and a call is made for the creation of mechanisms at all levels to achieve these objectives. Special attention is paid to health and nutrition, education, training for employment, and the particular needs of women among the rural and urban poor. States and international organizations are also

----

[1] Four States voted against the Programme: the United States, Canada, Australia, and Israel. Their representatives expressed the view that although they agreed with most of the Programme, they objected to the intrusion of "political" subjects into the consideration of the conference. They were particularly concerned about provisions which condemned zionism and urged support for Palestinian women through the Palestine Liberation Organization.

called upon to integrate women into the decision-making
structures of their institutions, especially those
dealing with development.

Summary

    The Programme is a lengthy document, with more
detailed guidelines and strategies than the World Plan.
It is divided into three major sections which provide a
general background statement, a plan for the national
level, and one for the regional and international levels.
    The introduction to Part I reviews the legislative
mandate for the Programme and the Copenhagen Conference,
making reference to the relevant United Nations
resolutions. There is an explication of the three themes
of the decade: equality, development, and peace, and a
statement of their interconnectedness. There is then a
discussion of the nature and scope of the Programme,
including the importance of the three subthemes:
employment, health, and education. A recommendation is
made that a second decade be planned.
    The entire Programme is placed in historical
perspective through a discussion of the causes of
inequality, with stress on the major theme of
development, and a linkage is drawn between the
political, economic, and social conditions of the world
and those of individual national societies. By reviewing
the advances as well as the obstacles to progress which
characterised the first half of the decade, the Programme
draws some basic lessons for the future. Its conclusions
are that although custom and tradition play an important
role in limiting the advancement of women, many of the
constraints are international and result from the
inequities existing between developed and developing
nations. A conceptual framework is then developed to
improve the collection and utilization of research
relevant to the objectives of the decade.
    Part II, which is devoted to action at the national
level, begins with a discussion of national targets and
strategies for the full participation of women in
economic and social development. The major focus here is
on accelerating the process of involving women in the
economic and social lives of their countries. Stress is
placed on attitudes and the need to involve men more
fully in family life, particularly in child-rearing. The
Programme provides specific targets and guidelines for
all levels of national activity in order to achieve the
basic objectives, with recommendations for political,
economic, legal, administrative, and social action.
Among the areas covered are education and dissemination
of information, improvement of the data base for research

and policy, involvement of nongovernmental organizations, and organizing grass-roots participation.

In a subsection, the Programme elaborates the specific action needed to repond to the subthemes. It identifies priority areas of responsibility; for example, with regard to employment, the Programme addresses the need to inform women workers of their rights, to include women in development planning activities at all levels, to safeguard women's work during pregnancy, to recognize and reward unpaid work in the household, to provide an infrastructure of services to facilitate work by women outside the household, to afford training programs to women for advancement, and to encourage more flexible working hours to accomodate women with families. Similar areas of priority action are identified with regard to the other two subthemes: health and education. There is a separate discussion of the special needs of rural women and priority areas of action to meet these needs. Other special discussions are devoted to child care, migrant women, unemployed women, women who head single parent households, and young women.

Part III is devoted to international and regional targets and strategies for the decade. Here again emphasis is laid on including women in the planning process and a call on the United Nations itself and its specialized agencies to take a more assertive role in advancing the status of women by addressing the needs of women by more active concern. Mention is made of the special relationship between women and underdevelopment and the general need for disarmament. The United Nations is called upon to coordinate programs of development with increased use of regional and multilateral planning. The Secretariat is urged to make legal and economic studies which would provide comparative data on the position of women in various countries and to suggest means of promoting equality between the sexes. Five special topics are discussed separately. The first, technical cooperation, training, and advisory services, includes: mobilization of human resources; assistance to women in southern Africa; assistance to the Palestinian women inside and outside the occupied territories; and assistance to women refugees and displaced women. The second focuses on the elaboration and review of international standards. The third highlights the need for improved collection and analysis of data related to women's needs. Further research at the regional and international levels is urged. The fourth topic is the dissemination of information and experience; here the United Nations is called upon to include women's issues in the existing data collection and dissemination systems. All the United Nations agencies and commissions are asked to include information about the decade in

their publications.   The fifth item is devoted to the
process of review and appraisal.   The United Nations
system is asked to carry out a comprehensive biennial
review of progress during the decade with analysis and
reporting of their conclusions.   Responsibility for this
process is placed with the Commission on the Status of
Women and the Branch for the Advancement of Women with a
request that   they be   expanded and   provided with
additional funding.
     A final brief portion of the report is devoted to
regional action with emphasis on the United Nations
regional commissions and specialized agencies.   Many of
the priorities suggested for the global level of action
are also stressed for regional programming.   Again the
need to recruit women into the higher levels of the
administration of the regional commissions is emphasized.

For a text of the Programme of Action in its entirety
see: United Nations, Report of the World Conference of
the   United Nations Decade   for Women: Equality,
Development and Peace, (New York: United Nations, 1980).
pp. 2-59.   U.N.Document A/Conf.94/35.

Summary Table of Ratifications

(See p.244 for legend)

Country	1	2	4	5	6	7	8	9	10	11	12	13	14	15	16	17	18	21
Afghanistan	R	R	R		R	R	R	R		R			R					S
Albania	R		R	R	R	S	R	R		R	R			R				
Algeria	R		R	R	R	R	R		R	R			R	R		S	S	
Angola	R	R	R			R							R					
Antigua and Barbuda	R																	
Argentina	R	R	R	R	S		R	R	R	R	R		R	R	R	S	S	S
Australia	R	R		R	R	R	R		R	R	R	R	R		R	R		S
Austria	R	R	R		R	R	R	R	R	R	R		R		R	R	R	R
Bahamas	R	R			R			R		R	R							
Bahrain	R	R		R														
Bangladesh	R	R	R										R					
Barbados	R					R	R		R	R			R	R	R	R	R	R
Belgium	R	R	R	R	R	R	R	R		R	J		ll			S	J	J
Belize	R																	
Benin	R		R			R	R						R	R	R			S
Bhutan	R																	R
Bolivia	R	R	R			R	R	R					R					S
Botswana	R																	
Brazil	R	R	R	R	R	R	R	R	R	R	R	R	R	R	R			S
Bulgaria	R	R	R	R	R	R	R	R	R	R	R		R	R		R	R	R
Burma	R		R	S	S			S										
Burundi	R		R															S
Byelorussian SSR	R	R		R	R	R	R	R	R	R	R		R	R		R	R	R
Canada	R	R			R		R	R		R	R		R			R	R	R
Cape Verde	R					R							R					R
Central African Republic	R		R	R		R	R	R	R	R			R	R		R	R	
Chad	R		R				R						R					
Chile	R	R	R			R	R	R	R		S		R	R	S	R	R	S
China	R	R			S	S	R	R		R	R		R	R	R	R	S	

- 240 -

	1	2	4	5	6	7	8	9	10	11	12	13	14	15	16	17	18	21
Colombia	R		R		R		R		R		S		R			R	R	R
Comoros	R	R			R													
Congo	R		R	R		R		R		R			R					S
Costa Rica	R	R	R		S		R	R					R	R		R	R	S
Cuba	R	R	R	R	R	R	R	R	R	R	R		R	R	R			R
Cyprus	R	R	R		R			R		R	R		R	R			R	R
Czechoslovakia	R	R	R	R	R	R	R	R		R	R		R	R	R	R	R	R
Democratic Kampuchea	R		R							R						S	S	S
Democratic People's Republic of Korea																R	R	
Democratic Yemen	R																	
Denmark	R			S	R		R	R		R	R		R	R	R	R	R	S
Djibouti	R	R	R	R	R					R								
Dominica	R																	R
Dominican Republic	R	R	R				R	R		R	R		R	R	R	R	R	S
Ecuador	R	R		R			R	R	R	R	R		R	R		R	R	R
Egypt (U. A. R.)	R	R	R	R	R		R	R		R			R	R		R	R	R
El Salvador	R						S		S							R	R	R
Ethiopia	R		R				R		R				R					R
Equatorial Guinea	R																	
Fiji	R	R		R			R		R	R				R				
Finland	R	R		R	R	R	R	R		R	R		R	R	R	R	R	S
France	R	R	R	R	R	R	R	R	R	R		R	R	R	S	R	R	S
Gabon	R	R	R				R	R	R				R					S
Gambia	R															R	R	S
German Democratic Republic	R	R		R	R	R	R	R	R	R	R		R	R	R	R	R	R
Germany, Federal Republic of	R	R			S		R	R	R	R	R		R	R	R	R	R	S
Ghana	R	R	R		R		R	R		R	R		R					S
Greece	R	R	R		R	R	R	R	R						S			
Grenada	R																	S
Guatemala	R	R	R				R	R		S	R	R	R					S
Guinea	R	R	R	R			R	R	R	R	S		R	R	R	R	R	S
Guinea-Bissau	R	R	R				R						R					S
Guyana	R	R					R						R			R	R	R
Haiti	R	R	R				R	R		R			R					R
Honduras	R	R	S				R						R			S	R	S
Hungary	R	R	R	R	R	R	R	R	R	R	R		R	R	R	R	R	S
Iceland	R						R	R		R	R		R		R	R	R	S
India	R	R	R	R	R		R	R		R	S		R			R	R	S
Indonesia	R	R					R	R							R			S
Iran	R			S	R	R	R			R			R	R		R	R	
Iraq	R		R	R	R		R			R			R	R		R	R	
Ireland	R	R	R		R	R	R	R		R	R		R			S	S	
Israel	R			R			R	R		R	R		R	R	S	S	S	S

- 241 -

	1	2	4	5	6	7	8	9	10	11	12	13	14	15	16	17	18	21
Italy	R	R	R	R	R		R	R	R	R		R	R	R	S	R	R	S
Ivory Coast	R	R	R			R	R		R	R		R						S
Jamaica	R			R		R	R		R	R						R	R	S
Japan	R	R		R	R		R	R								R	R	S
Jordan	R			R			R			R			R	R		R	R	S
Kenya	R	R	R													R	R	
Kuwait	R		R	R						R			R	R				
Lao People's Democratic Republic	R		R	R				R		R								R
Lebanon	R	R	R		S		R	R				R	R		R	R		
Lesotho	R	R					R		R	R								R
Liberia	R		S				S		S				R	R		S	S	
Libyan Arab Jamahiriya	R		R	R	R	R	R		R				R	R		R	R	
Luxembourg	R	R	R	S	R	R	R	R	R	R	R				R		S	S
Madagascar	R		R		R	R	R	R		R			R	R		R	R	S
Malawi	R	R	R	R	R		R	R		R	R		R					
Malaysia	R	R								R	R							
Maldives	R																	
Mali	R		R	R		R	R	R		R	R		R		R	R	R	
Malta	R		R		R			R		R	R		R	R			S	
Mauritania	R		R					R	R				R					
Mauritius	R				R			R		R	R			R		R	R	
Mexico	R	R		R	R	R	R	R		R	R	R	R			R	R	R
Mongolia	R						R	R	R	R		R	R		R	R	R	R
Morocco	R	R	R	R			R	R		R		R	R		R	R		
Mozambique	R						R			R			R					
Nepal	R						R	R		R			R					
Netherlands	R	R	R		R	R	R	R	R	R		R	R	R	R	R	R	S
New Zealand	R	R	R		R			R		R	R			R	R	R	R	C
Nicaragua	R	R	R			R	R	R	R	R			R			R	R	R
Niger	R		R	R		R	R	R		R			R	R	R			
Nigeria	R	R					R	R		R				R				
Norway	R			R	R	R	R	R		R	R	R	R	R	R	R	R	R
Oman	R																	
Pakistan	R	R	R	R	R			R		R	R	S		R				
Panama	R	R	R		S	S	R		R				R	R		R	R	R
Papua New Guinea	R	R						R		R								
Paraguay	R		R				R	S					R					
Peru	R	R	R		S			R		S			R	R		R	R	S
Philippines	R		R	R	R	R	R	R		R			R	R	R	S	R	R
Poland	R	R		R	R	R	R	R	R	R	R		R	R	R	R	R	R
Portugal	R	R	R		R	R	R			R	S	R	R		R	R		
Qatar	R												R					
Republic of Korea					R			R										
Romania	R		R	R	R	R	R	R	R	R		R	R	S	R	R	R	
Rwanda	R		R				R			R					R	R	R	
Saint Lucia	R																	

	1	2	4	5	6	7	8	9	10	11	12	13	14	15	16	17	18	21
Saint Vincent and the Grenadines	R								R							R	R	R
Samoa	R														R			
Sao Tome and Principe	R																	
Saudi Arabia	R	R	R			R			R				R	R				
Senegal	R		R	R		R	R	R	R				R	R		R	R	S
Seychelles	R																	
Sierra Leone	R	R			R		R	R		R	R		R	R				
Singapore	R	R		R	R	R				R	R							
Solomon Islands	R						R		R									
Somalia	R	R											R					
South Africa (Union of South Africa)	R	R	R	R	R	R												
Spain	R	R	R	R	R	S	R	R	R	R		R	R	R	R	R	R	S
Sri Lanka	R	R	R	R					R	R					S	R	R	R
Sudan	R				R	R	R		R				R					
Suriname	R		R						R							R	R	
Swaziland	R	R	R				R	R		R			R	R				
Sweden	R	R			R	R	R	R	R	R			R	R	R	R	R	R
Switzerland		R	R		R	R							R					
Syrian Arab Republic	R	R	R	R	S		R		R				R			R	R	
Thailand	R				R			R										
Togo	R		R						R									
Trinidad and Tobago	R							R	R	R			R			R	R	R
Tunisia	R	R	R				R	R	R	R			R	R	R	R	R	S
Turkey	R	R			R	R	R	R	R				R					
Uganda	R	R							R	R				R				S
Ukrainian SSR	R	R		R			R	R	R	R			R	R		R	R	R
Union of Soviet Socialist Republics	R	R		R	R	R	R	R	R	R				R		R	R	R
United Arab Emirates	R																	
United Kingdom of Great Britain and N. Ireland	R	R	R		R	S	R	R		R	R				R	R	R	S
United Republic of Cameroon	R	R	R	R		R	R		R									
United Republic of Tanzania	R		R					R		R	R			R		R	R	S
Tanganyika	R																	

- 243 -

	1	2	4	5	6	7	8	9	10	11	12	13	14	15	16	17	18	21
Zanzibar	R																	
United States of America	R						R		R							S	S	S
Upper Volta	R		R	R		R	R						R		R			
Uruguay	R	R	R		R		S	R		S						R	R	R
Vanuatu	R																	
Venezuela	R	R	R	R				R					R	R		R	R	S
Viet Nam	R	R	R						S				R	R				R
Yemen	R					R							R					
Yugoslavia	R	R	R	R	R	S	R	R	R	R	R	R	R	R	R	R	R	R
Zaire	R		R			R	R	R								R	R	S
Zambia	R	R	R		R		R	R	R	R	R		R					S
Zimbabwe	R	R																

"R" indicates ratification or accession.

"S" indicates signature only.

1. Charter of the United Nations
2. Underground Mines Convention
4. Night Work (Women) Convention
5. Traffic in Persons Convention
6. Traffic in Women and Children Convention
7. Traffic in Women of Full Age Convention
8. Equal Remuneration Convention
9. Political Rights of Women Convention
10. Maternity Protection Convention
11. Supplementary Slavery Convention
12. Nationality of Married Women Convention
13. Plantation Workers Convention
14. Discrimination (Employment and Occupation) Convention
15. Discrimination in Education Convention
16. Marriage Convention
17. Civil and Political Rights Covenant
18. Economic, Social and Cultural Rights Covenant
21. Convention on the Elimination of All Forms of
    Discrimination Against Women

Index

apartheid, 203, 208, 209

Babcock, B., 8 fn., 10 fn., 18 fn.

Baxter, M.K. 13 fn.9

Charter of the United Nations, See United Nations, Charter

Chen, L., 3 fn.

Civil and Political Rights Covenant, 14-15, 40 fn., 183-188, 194, 217
background, 183
table of ratifications, 187-188
text (excerpts), 184-187

colonialism, 3 fn., 203, 208, 209

Commission on Human Rights, 63, 156, 183

Commission on the Status of Women, 13 fn., 23, 34, 50, 50 fn., 103, 112, 142-143, 194, 240

Committee on the Elimination of Discrimination Against Women, 34-35, 229-232

Convention Against Discrimination in Education, See Discrimination in Education Convention

Convention Concerning Conditions of Employment of

Plantation Workers, See Plantation Workers Convention

Convention Concerning Discrimination in Respect of Employment and Occupation, See Discrimination (Employment and Occupation) Convention

Convention Concerning Employment of Women on Underground Work in Mines of All Kinds, See Underground Mines Convention

Convention Concerning Equal Remuneration for Men and Women Workers for Work of Equal Value, See Equal Remuneration Convention

Convention Concerning Maternity Protection, See Maternity Protection Convention

Convention Concerning Night Work of Women Employed in Industry, See Night Work Convention

Convention for the Suppression of the Traffic in Persons and of the Exploitation and of the Prostitution of Others, See Traffic in Persons Convention